Cheers!

Jake

BBQ PIZZA

A FLAMING EXPOSÉ ON MACHO COOKING

Gabriella Owens

Legal Disclaimer

This book features stunts performed by amateurs not under the supervision of professionals. Due to the dangers of combining open flames with alcohol, the author must insist that no one attempt to re-create or re-enact any stunt or activity performed in this book. (Whew! Now I'm safe from singed nose hair lawsuits!)

ISBN-13: 978-1484165430

ISBN-10: 1484165438

This work began as almost factual with additions, embellishments, embroidering and large doses of poetic license knitted together until it became a complete fabrication with no resemblance to reality. All names, characters, locations and incidents were altered to expose as many undergarments as possible. Any resemblance to actual events is totally intentional, but the truth has been exaggerated, twisted and tortured until such actual events should be entirely unrecognizable.

No life-threatening injuries were sustained during the creation of this book and all participants have gone on to lead somewhat productive lives. Unfortunately Brian's nose hairs did grow back, a fact which his sixth grade students remark on frequently.

Acknowledgements

I want to thank all my friends and family for being such good sports. The only thing better than making fun of my husband is getting to make fun of several husbands and assorted other folks as well. Like a bowl of mixed nuts, each one adds its own peculiar flavoring.

Special thanks to all the wonderful people who helped with this book. First I have to thank my husband Greg, without him none of this would be possible. Love you sweetie!

Rick and Marianne have been fantastic! How many best friends would let someone turn their husband into a comedic character? (Yes, the final decision is always the wife's. Don't you forget that!)

The wildly famous Jack Russo created the magnificent cartoons for me. Yvonne arranged the photographs from which the illustrations were done. Steve and Yolanda critiqued my writing and encouraged me to keep going. Grace and so many other family members and friends have made suggestions, tested recipes and edited text. I am so grateful for all their help! Without them this book would not exist. Thank you all!

Table of Contents

How This Whole Thing Got Started

Every journey begins with a single step. If that step leads over a cliff most sensible people don't embark. We jumped. Our best friends, Rick and Marianne, introduced us to barbecued pizza.

We all met when my husband Greg and Marianne's husband Rick became leaders of the Boy Scout troop together. Basically when you put these two guys together you have Tim Allen, John Cleese and Peter Sellers all rolled into one. The two of them get into more trouble than three people, and not even normal people at that. Thankfully all the scouts survived their leadership and have grown into responsible adults despite the experience.

So, true to tradition, the two guys barbequing a pizza together was not exactly a resounding success the first time out, or even the fourth, but I get ahead of myself. Their first pizza attempt was more of a Laurel and Hardy "fine mess."

Problem number one – the pizza did not want to be cooked and clung tenaciously to the baking sheet it had been assembled on. It took all four of us to dislodge it. One of us held the sheet, another worked two spatulas under the center of it and the others grabbed the edges with their fingers.

The pizza, which had been a minor work of art before this process, finally ended up on the grill looking considerably worse for wear. I'd say like preschool finger painting, but that still implies some level of artistic merit.

Which brings me to problem number two – they cooked the pizza directly on the grill. This was such a colossal error that even our intrepid adventurers never attempted to do so again. Problem number three compounded error number two. They cooked the pizza for the length of time recommended for a pizza in a 350 degree oven.

Macho cooking rule number one is to never use an oven when unregulated flames are available. Rick, at this point, was a hard core macho cooker. No wimpy gas barbeques for him. He was strictly a charcoal or hard wood barbequer.

Now in an oven, the pizza is probably a good eight inches away from the heat source. On a barbeque it might be two, unless Greg and Rick are involved. The more heat the better, is the second rule of macho cooking, so they lowered the rack until it was almost touching the coals. Once the coals were heated to an unknown temperature, somewhere between scorching and hell, they began cooking pizza.

Macho cookers (like hookers only with a "c") don't need to measure the temperature. If you can't comfortably stand within five feet of the barbeque, then it is ready. They intended to cook the pizza for twenty minutes, but thankfully after about ten minutes, they got tired of listening to their wives complain about the smoke billowing out of the barbeque and decided to check on the pizza. It was, predictably, a burnt offering to the gods of macho cooking.

Since they were not expecting the pizza to be done so quickly, they had nothing to remove the pizza with and nothing to put it on either. After a quick keystone cops drill to acquire the necessary tools the pizza was removed from the barbeque and displayed in all its glory. The bottom was black with gray stripes where the charcoal crust had begun to turn to ash. It looked more like something unearthed from the ruins of Pompeii than something edible.

On a positive note, most of the toppings were protected by a heavy layer of pesto sauce and were therefore still edible. Since all we could eat were the toppings, we scraped them off using crackers as both utensils and dinner. The boys will try to claim credit for the wondrous invention of the world famous Pizza Dip, but this historically significant creation was not their idea. Marianne thought of it. The artichoke hearts, chopped pepperoni and sundried tomatoes swimming in melted mozzarella were simply delicious. It would have been a wonderful pizza if the gods of macho cooking hadn't cooked it to death.

After a disaster like this most reasonable people would go back to buying their pizzas from Vincenzo's and give up on cooking them themselves – let alone barbequing pizzas. However macho cooks would not survive Boy Scouts if they gave up after the first, or forty seventh, inedible meal. After a dozen years of teenage boys cooking meals on hikes and campouts, eating something that is blackened so badly that it is impossible to identify what it was in the first place is just commonplace.

Greg and Rick were convinced that if they could master the process of barbequing pizzas the results would be worth it. So they began experimenting. Having their wives express doubts only added to their determination.

Recommended Equipment

If you are going to barbeque pizzas you will need a barbeque. This should be obvious, but people are always asking if you can use an oven instead. Of course you can cook pizzas in an oven, but if you do then you aren't a real macho cook. Barbequed pizza is man food. Oven cooked is for wimps. You also heat up the house using an oven and are not enjoying the great outdoors.

The barbeque should have a grill large enough for at least one pizza stone with a few inches on every side. Gas barbeques are much easier to work with than wood or charcoal. The barbeque must also have a lid to keep heat in.

We have found that pizzas cook best on a pizza stone. It is possible to cook them on the grill itself as long as the heat source (burner or coals) is not directly below the pizza. To start with you can buy an inexpensive stone available at most department or kitchen stores for around $15.

As you become hooked on barbequing pizzas, you will need a sturdier stone. Check with countertop suppliers for soapstone remnants that are a couple of inches smaller than your barbecue's grill . You want something big enough for a pizza or two, but small enough to allow hot air to circulate up from the burners. Good heat circulation is needed to cook the toppings.

Do NOT use concrete or porous stones. If moisture can penetrate or be absorbed by the stone then when the stone is heated steam pressure could theoretically explode the stone.

Some way to monitor the temperature of the barbeque and the stone is helpful. Many barbeques have a thermometer on the lid which is probably all you really need. (Actually you could even judge the cooking by whether the cheese is melted and the crust is brown.) Just preheat the stone for long enough to bring its temperature up to the ambient barbeque temperature.

If you prefer to have an excuse for gadget shopping then a Heat Sensing Gun or Infrared Laser Thermometer would make it possible to accurately measure the temperature of the stone itself. On sale they can be found in the $20 to $30 range.

You will want to have several wood pizza peels for assembling and carrying pizzas and one metal peel for turning the pizzas while they are on the barbeque. Pizza peels are flat shovel shaped boards. Metal peels are thin and therefore easier to slide under a cooking pizza, but pizzas also slide off metal peels more easily, so metal peels are not the best for carrying pizzas from the barbeque to the table. (Always turn and walk slowly when carrying pizzas, they like to jump off all kinds of peels.)

A mixer with dough hooks is very handy. However, you can knead dough by hand, especially if you want to build hand and arm strength and save on gym fees. You will want a couple of large mixing bowls for making dough in. Baking sheets are handy for the second rising of the dough. You will also want a rolling pin for rolling out dough.

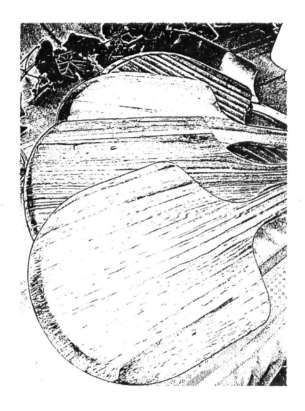

Several cutting boards will be needed. At least two large ones, one for rolling out dough and the second for cutting cooked pizzas. Do not cut pizzas on the peels, it roughens up the peel surface and makes pizzas stick. You will also want a small cutting board or two to chop ingredients on.

A pizza cutter or two for cutting pizzas is nice. You'll also need the normal knives, measuring cups and spoons, wineglasses and corkscrews that every kitchen has. (Wineglasses are essential tools for pizza making.)

Wine Pairings

When you pair really good food with really good wine or beer, you get something more than the sum of the parts. (Two plus two can equal five!) The flavors in one can enhance the flavors of the other, making for a much more enjoyable meal. However, if you choose flavors that don't match well then you may find one overpowers the other or they clash terribly. (Two plus two is now only one.)

Here it comes, the single most important piece of advice in the entire book: Should this happen set the bottle aside to try with something different and open another bottle. Repeat until you are happy with the results.

For each of the pizzas in this book our group of friends has helped us select a good wine or beer to have with it. Do we know what we are doing? For most of this book I have gone to great lengths to convince you that we don't have a clue. However, I must point out that as a group, we have hundreds of years and thousands of gallons of experience with alcohol consumption to base our opinions on.

Not impressed? Hmmm. Does it help that some of us are wine and beer makers? Perhaps I should add successful to that statement? Some of our gang actually have won medals in wine competition. Better? We also have a few wine judges in the group as well.

However, you should NOT follow our recommendations blindly. Each and every one of us has our own likes and dislikes. Greg likes big, bold wines such as Cabernet Sauvignon. He says anything you can see through is a Rosé. I prefer light, sweet fruity wines. Our sons like microbrew ales.

As you taste different beers and wines, you will notice differences between brewers and winemakers. Some wines have a lot of fruit flavors, others have more earthy notes. Some winemakers make wines with strong tannins from the skins and oak. The fun of wine is discovering on your own which combinations of these flavors that you like best. Use our suggestions as a starting point, if you don't find the exact wine, look for one made from the same grape or in a similar style.

We live in Southern California and are only a few hours away from Paso Robles, which is one of the world's best wine regions. (Did I mention that I am opinionated?) We have spent years exploring the different wineries with our friends and we have many favorites. Paso is a wonderful place to visit. The people are friendly, the wines top notch and the country is beautiful.

We have even taken our pizza making party on the road up to Paso. We always stay in the La Quinta, the best hotel in Paso. (Shameless promotion! You are welcome Vic!) The staff is friendly, they welcome our little dogs and they have free wine tasting on weekday evenings.

One Monday afternoon we commandeered the hotel's barbeque. (When Vic reads this book, he will realize the risk he took!) We set up folding tables in the parking lot and had a great time with all our friends from the hotel staff and local tasting rooms. We had brought all the fixings in disposable containers so clean up was pretty easy.

Up (or Down) in Flames

Macho cooks are never wrong. No matter how obvious it is to the rest of the world. If their charcoal barbeque is not good for cooking pizzas this is a fact they will never agree to. That barbeque worked just fine. It was the type of dough that caused the problem, or the women put too many (or few) toppings on to be able to cook it properly. The wind coming out of the west unexpectedly fanned the coals to a sudden high flame or the full moon threw dark, dancing shadows on the pizza.

If a wife is foolish enough to voice any doubts about the barbeque itself, then the macho cook will rise to the defense of his equipment and pizza cooking will be done on that barbeque until the end of time. A macho man (Do I hear the Village People's song? Macho, macho man, I've got to be a macho man...) never, ever admits any fault in his equipment to his wife.

However if another macho cook should suggest using a different barbeque, then the first macho cook will drop his current barbeque like a hot potato. The barbeque improvements that will prompt the purchase of another barbeque are always bigger, hotter, faster, and more room for food on the grill. The same sort of features that attract them to cars and sports teams.

Macho cooks are attracted to shiny grills and need a new one more often than their wife gets diamonds. Our macho cooks came up with the idea that new barbeques might be better for pizzas, so both our macho cooks went shopping.

There is no noticeable difference between a kid in a candy store or a guy in a home improvement store. Unless you count the amount of money they can spend. Kids usually have only a handful of coins, guys have plastic.

When the salesman saw our two guys walk through the door he knew this was his day. With starry eyes and tongues hanging out of their mouths the two bargain hunters gazed at row upon row of gleaming stainless steel barbeques. With a little mention of sear burners here and zero to four hundred in seconds there, the salesman soon steered our savvy shoppers to the most expensive, over-priced models.

Greg brought home what I call the "Binford 9000" barbeque. It was the largest barbeque available for sale on the West Coast. This thing has a grill the size of a football field, five huge burners that take up every inch of space under that grill, and a British Thermal Unit (BTU) rating that includes Ireland and Wales. The gauge on the lid is supposed to read the temperature, but basically it registers maximum right after lighting up the burners, making it just an "on" indicator.

My husband and our two sons gathered around the new macho cooking shrine for the ceremonial first firing and quickly learned a lesson about opening the lid with all burners on maximum. DON'T! It singed off all their arm hair on one arm each, two lefts and a right.

Now when the first son opened the lid and singed his hair you would expect the other guys to learn from this. No, the second son reached over the barbeque to close the lid and singed the hair off of one of his arms too. He was also laughing at his brother when he leaned over the grill, and so inhaled deeply through his nose, singeing his nose hairs at the same time.

At this point Greg notices the smell of smoldering hair and worries that something inside the barbeque is going wrong. So he opens the lid again, singeing yet another arm. Did they then think to turn the barbeque off before leaning back over it to investigate the smell of burning hair? No. I had to yell at them to keep them from losing their eyebrows.

What possessed me at that point, I really don't know. I should have just grabbed a video camera. Could have made a fortune on America's Funniest Videos. Is it women's maternal instincts and compassion that hold us back? If we would just leave men alone and stop saving them from their follies we could be on top of the world.

The guys seemed to think that the fact that some of the burners were improperly assembled, and putting out exponentially more heat than they were supposed to, makes them sound less stupid. Hello! They were the ones who assembled it wrong in the first place. And then tested it at full heat under a wooden patio cover with the gas meter spinning like a pinwheel. Greg still hasn't painted over the scorch marks on the patio.

Two of these guys are engineers and the third is a teacher – so if by some quirk of fate civilization does not collapse under the influence of the first two, it is likely to implode when the next generation takes over. If you look back over history you will see that with each generation the capacity for disaster has increased. My husband and sons are doing everything they can to accelerate this process.

Not to be outdone by Greg's purchase, Rick bought two barbeques which together are larger than the grill size of the Binford 9000. Macho cooks cannot have smaller barbequing equipment than their buddies have. It just isn't done.

One of Rick's new barbeques was a shiny new charcoal grill and the other was a cute little gas barbeque just big enough for one pizza at a time. Both these barbeques were designed to be free standing barbeques.

The two macho cooks spent hours drinking wine and discussing the placement of these two barbeques before coming up with a brilliant idea. They would build them into a big bar with a marble counter top. Why? Because alcohol should always be stored in close proximity to open flame. (Is it open flame if the barbeque has a lid? The guys seemed to think not.)

The construction of this bar took an entire summer. Every weekend Greg would go over to Rick's and they would "work" on the bar. After half an hour of actual labor, they would take a break, have a beer or a glass of wine and any visible progress would essentially cease for the day.

About the time that the weather became cool enough that an evening outside by the barbeque would no longer be pleasant, they were finally finished. So an inaugural party to barbeque pizzas on Rick's new grill was planned. Rick was eager to recapture his macho cooking image after the Pompeii pizza debacle.

The gas barbeque was fired up and cooking commenced with many compliments on the efficiency of his new grill, plenty of alcohol and lots of macho grunting. The first pizza came out just fine. Rick had his macho swagger back and was enjoying his wine and the envy of his buddies.

Somewhere during the second pizza, people began to notice a bit too much smoke from the barbeque. Rick turned the heat down and cleaned the old burned corn meal off the pizza stone. Instead of dissipating, the amount of smoke increased alarmingly.

Soon the macho cooks began yelling, waving their arms wildly and brought out the garden hose. In true Marx Brother's fashion, they drenched the barbeque, the bar, the cupboard under the bar, and any guest standing within ten feet. The pizza that had been cooking was a waterlogged mess.

The bar was saved, although portions of the cupboard beneath were badly scorched. It turns out that freestanding barbeques are not designed to be built in, (Duh!) and have no barriers to keep heat and flame from igniting two by fours or plywood that are placed in close proximity to the bottom or sides of such a barbeque.

The barbeque builders spent the next few weekends contemplating this revelation. Consuming copious quantities of alcohol while bemoaning Rick's bad luck. "Luck," not planning. These are macho construction guys. Nothing that goes wrong with something they have built is ever their fault.

Like the builders of the unsinkable Titanic, they believe their planning and execution were flawless, despite the amount of alcohol involved or the ultimate result. Eventually these incomparable architects arrived at a solution and rebuilt the bar, keeping flammable materials away from the barbeques.

Dough Recipes

You'll want to make your dough on the morning of, or the day before, you plan on having pizzas. Dough is best made fresh the same day several hours before cooking, allowing for it to rise twice.

The recipes that follow will make three or four thin crust pizzas each. Typically you should use one cup of flour for each pizza you want to make. If you prefer thicker crusts then change the math accordingly.

Since these are fairly small pizzas, most people will eat half to one pizza each. When it is just the family or a small group I usually make enough dough for one pizza per person. That way everyone can make what they want and there will be leftover pizza to snack on the next day.

Balls of dough that you are not going to cook the same day can be put in plastic Ziploc sandwich bags and stored in the fridge for up to 3 days or a few weeks in the freezer. Let dough warm to room temperature before using or it will be sticky and hard to roll – at least one hour for refrigerated and two or more for frozen. Turn the bag inside out and just hold it over a floured board, the dough will pull away from the plastic fairly easily.

Basic White Pizza Dough

This recipe is about enough dough for four thin crust pizzas. Pizzas vary quite a bit in size and shape, depending on the skill of the person rolling them out. Expect them to be somewhere around 11 or 12 inches across.

4 1/2 Cups Flour
1 1/2 Teaspoons Salt
2 Tablespoons Olive Oil (Variation: Use a garlic infused olive oil instead of plain olive oil.)
1 3/4 Cups Warm Water
1 Teaspoon Yeast (or 1 Packet)
1/2 Teaspoon Sugar
Oil Spray

Dissolve yeast and sugar in water. (If you are not sure how old the yeast is wait and see that it starts bubbling within a few minutes. If it doesn't the yeast is no good.) Mix the salt, oil and flour in. I use a mixer with dough hooks to mix and knead the dough. Knead for about 10 minutes until smooth.

Spray the dough with the oil spray and cover the bowl with plastic wrap to keep the dough from drying and getting crusty. Let the dough rise until about double in size, usually at least a couple of hours. Longer rising times makes better dough. Dough rises best in warm conditions, so keep it away from drafts.

You can knead the dough every hour or two for better consistency. I have never found the time to do this. I just let it rise most of the day, then knead it a little just before dividing.

Dump the dough out onto a well floured board, kneed the dough for several minutes. Then divide into four equal pieces (each about softball size). Place on a floured board or sheet, spray tops with oil spray and cover with plastic wrap again. The dough will roll out easier if left to rest and rise for half an hour or more after dividing.

When you are ready to cook pizzas, roll each ball of dough out on a floured board, gently shake off extra flour and transfer to a pizza peel with corn meal on it to prevent sticking.

Beer Pizza Dough

3 1/2 Cups Flour
1 Teaspoon Salt
2 Tablespoons Olive Oil
1 12 ounce Warm Beer
1 Teaspoon Yeast (or 1 Packet)

1/2 Teaspoon Sugar
Oil Spray

Make sure the beer is at least at room temperature. I leave the beer out overnight before making beer dough. If it is a cool day gently warm the beer in the bowl in the oven on the lowest temperature until it is warm but not hot.

Dissolve yeast, salt and sugar in beer. Mix the oil and flour in. I use a mixer with dough hooks to mix and knead the dough. Knead for about 10 minutes until smooth.

Spray the dough with the oil spray and cover the bowl with plastic wrap to keep the dough from drying and getting crusty. Let the dough rise until about double in size, usually at least a couple of hours. Longer rising times makes better dough. Dough rises best in warm conditions, so keep it away from drafts.

You can knead the dough every hour or two for better consistency. I have never found the time to do this. I just let it rise most of the day, then knead it a little just before dividing.

Dump the dough out onto a well floured board, kneed the dough for several minutes. Then divide into three equal pieces (each about softball size). Place on a floured board or sheet, spray tops with oil spray and cover with plastic wrap again. The dough will roll out easier if left to rest and rise for half an hour or more after dividing.

When you are ready to cook pizzas, roll each ball of dough out on a floured board, gently shake off extra flour and transfer to a pizza peel with corn meal on it to prevent sticking.

Dessert Pizza Dough

This dough is sweeter than regular dough, but the sugar also makes it burn much more easily, so cook it at lower temperatures. The almond meal adds a nice nutty flavor, and makes the dough heavier which helps with the gooier toppings.

4 Cups Flour
1 Cup Almond Meal
1 1/2 Teaspoons Salt
1 Tablespoon Olive Oil (Variation: Use an orange infused olive oil instead of plain olive oil.)
1 1/2 Cups Warm Water
1 Teaspoon Yeast (or 1 Packet)
1 Cup Sugar
2 Tablespoons Vanilla
1 Tablespoon Cinnamon
Oil Spray

Dissolve yeast and sugar in water. (If you are not sure how old the yeast is wait and see that it starts bubbling within a few minutes. If it doesn't the yeast is no good.) Mix the salt, oil, vanilla, cinnamon, almond meal and flour in. I use a mixer with dough hooks to mix and knead the dough. Knead for about 10 minutes until smooth.

Spray the dough with the oil spray and cover the bowl with plastic wrap to keep the dough from drying and getting crusty. Let the dough rise until about double in size, usually at least a couple of hours. Longer rising times makes better dough. Dough rises best in warm conditions, so keep it away from drafts.

You can knead the dough every hour or two for better consistency. I have never found the time to do this. I just let it rise most of the day, then knead it a little just before dividing.

Dump the dough out onto a well floured board, kneed the dough for several minutes. Then divide into four equal pieces (each about softball size). Place on a floured board or sheet, spray tops with oil spray and cover with plastic wrap again. The dough will roll out easier if left to rest and rise for half an hour or more after dividing.

When you are ready to cook pizzas, roll each ball of dough out on a floured board, gently shake off extra flour and transfer to a pizza peel with corn meal on it to prevent sticking.

Herb Pizza Dough

Fresh chopped garlic tastes really good in the dough, but it can interfere with the yeast, so add it sparingly, just a tablespoon at the beginning. If you like a stronger garlic flavor, add 2 tablespoons after the dough has risen while kneading and dividing.

4 1/2 Cups Flour
1 1/2 Teaspoons Salt
2 Tablespoons Olive Oil
1 3/4 Cups Warm Water
1 Teaspoon Yeast (or 1 Packet)
1/2 Teaspoon Sugar
1 Tablespoon Italian Spice Mix (or a teaspoon each of oregano, basil, and thyme)

1 Tablespoon Minced Garlic
Oil Spray

Dissolve yeast and sugar in water. (If you are not sure how old the yeast is wait and see that it starts bubbling within a few minutes. If it doesn't the yeast is no good.) Mix the salt, oil, spices, garlic and flour in. I use a mixer with dough hooks to mix and knead the dough. Knead for about 10 minutes until smooth.

Spray the dough with the oil spray and cover the bowl with plastic wrap to keep the dough from drying and getting crusty. Let the dough rise until about double in size, usually at least a couple of hours. Longer rising times makes better dough. Dough rises best in warm conditions, so keep it away from drafts.

You can knead the dough every hour or two for better consistency. I have never found the time to do this. I just let it rise most of the day, then knead it a little just before dividing.

Dump the dough out onto a well floured board, kneed the dough for several minutes. Then divide into four equal pieces (each about softball size). Place on a floured board or sheet, spray tops with oil spray and cover with plastic wrap again. The dough will roll out easier if left to rest and rise for half an hour or more after dividing.

When you are ready to cook pizzas, roll each ball of dough out on a floured board, gently shake off extra flour and transfer to a pizza peel with corn meal on it to prevent sticking.

Whole Wheat Pizza Dough

Whole wheat flour absorbs more moisture and makes a heavier dough. So I prefer to use a mix of half whole wheat and half regular flour. Adjust the mixture to your own taste, just remember that when substituting whole wheat flour for regular flour you need to cut back a little on the quantity.

2 Cups Whole Wheat Flour
2 Cups Regular Flour
1 1/2 Teaspoons Salt
2 Tablespoon Olive Oil
1 3/4 Cups Warm Water
1 Teaspoon Yeast (1 Packet)
1/2 Teaspoon Sugar
Oil Spray

Dissolve yeast and sugar in water. (If you are not sure how old the yeast is wait and see that it starts bubbling within a few minutes. If it doesn't the yeast is no good.) Mix the salt, oil and both flours in. I use a mixer with dough hooks to mix and knead the dough. Knead for about 10 minutes until smooth.

Spray the dough with the oil spray and cover the bowl with plastic wrap to keep the dough from drying and getting crusty. Let the dough rise until about double in size, usually at least a couple of hours. Longer rising times makes better dough. Dough rises best in warm conditions, so keep it away from drafts.

You can knead the dough every hour or two for better consistency. I have never found the time to do this. I just let it rise most of the day, then knead it a little just before dividing.

Dump the dough out onto a well floured board, kneed the dough for several minutes. Then divide into four equal pieces (each about softball size). Place on a floured board or sheet, spray tops with oil spray and cover with plastic wrap again. The dough will roll out easier if left to rest and rise for half an hour or more after dividing.

When you are ready to cook pizzas, roll each ball of dough out on a floured board, gently shake off extra flour and transfer to a pizza peel with corn meal on it to prevent sticking.

Sauce Recipes

Just about any sauce imaginable can be used on pizza. The trick is combining the sauce with the right cheeses and toppings. So many sauces can easily be bought readymade and most of the time we just use sauces from the store.

When shopping for sauces, try to find sauces that do not have a lot of added sugar or salt. Instead look for sauces that get most of their flavor from other ingredients and spices. Because many cheeses and toppings like pepperoni are already high in salt, extra salt in the sauce can make a pizza too salty to eat.

If you decide to make your own sauces you'll want to make them ahead of time. Most sauces will keep for several days in the refrigerator and even longer in the freezer. Since each pizza uses only a few tablespoons of sauce, freeze extra sauce in small containers for future pizza making.

Alfredo Sauce

1/2 Cup Romano Cheese
1/2 Cup Parmesan Cheese
2 Cups Heavy Cream
1/2 Cup Butter
1 or 2 Cloves of Garlic, Minced
1/2 Teaspoon Pepper

Melt butter with garlic on medium heat. Mix in cream and then the cheeses. Add pepper to taste. Simmer for 5 to 10 minutes, stirring occasionally.

Chimichurri Sauce

1 Cup Fresh Italian Parsley
1 Teaspoon Basil, Thyme or Oregano
1/2 Cup Olive Oil
2 Tablespoons Lemon Juice
2 Shallots
1 Garlic Clove

Finely mince the shallots, garlic, parsley and herbs. Add the oil and lemon juice. Mix until smooth. Easiest to make using a food processor, but can be done by hand also. Keeps for a week or so in the refrigerator.

Fruit Compote

1/2 Cup Water
2 Cups Fresh or Frozen Berries
1/2 Cup Sugar

Bring water and fruit to a boil over high heat, stirring frequently. Lower heat to medium or medium low. Add sugar. Simmer, stirring frequently, until sauce begins to thicken, about 30 minutes. Strawberries tend to foam and boil over, so if using them, watch the sauce closely.

Marianne's (OMG I'm out of) Pizza Sauce

15 Ounce Can Tomato Sauce
1 Teaspoon Basil
1 Teaspoon Oregano
1/2 Teaspoon Salt
1/2 Teaspoon Pepper

Open the can. Mix in the spices. Spread on dough. It doesn't get any easier than this. Even a macho cook can make it.

Gabe's version

Well, this started out with Marianne's recipe, but it went through a few adjustments, which I believe were clearly implied. So, once again I have taken something and twisted it beyond recognition. Sorry Mare!

2 Cloves Garlic, Finely Chopped
1/2 of an Onion, Minced
1 Tablespoon Olive Oil
15 Ounce Can Tomato Sauce
6 Ounce Can Tomato Paste
1 Teaspoon Basil
1 Teaspoon Oregano
1/2 Teaspoon Salt
1/2 Teaspoon Pepper

In a large skillet, sauté the garlic and onion in olive oil at medium heat until the onion is clear. Lower the heat to low. Add the remaining ingredients and simmer for 10 minutes, stirring occasionally. For the macho cooks out there: Open the cans and only put the contents in the skillet. Discard the cans.

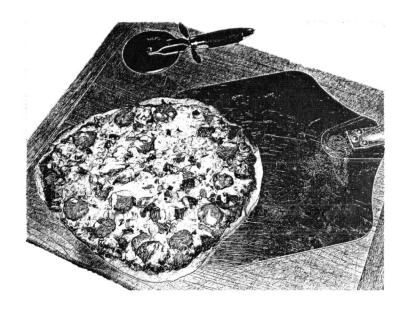

Pesto Sauce

Most store bought pesto sauces contain salt, which I try to avoid. If you top salty pesto sauce with salty toppings like pepperoni, then the salt becomes overpowering. Basil is easy to grow and so we have taken to making our own pesto when we have time. Thanks to Robin and Mark for the recipe!

1 Cup Fresh Basil Leaves
1/4 Cup Grated Parmesan or Romano Cheese
1/4 Cup Olive Oil

2 Tablespoons Pine Nuts or Walnuts
1 Garlic Clove

Finely mince the basil, garlic, and pine nuts. Add the oil and mix until smooth. Add the grated cheese and mix well. Easiest to make using a food processor, but can be done by hand also. Keeps for a week or so in the refrigerator.

Wine Reduction Sauce

1 Bottle Red Wine (Syrah, Zinfandel or ?)
1/4 Cup Honey
1/4 Cup Balsamic Vinegar
1 Clove of Garlic, Lightly Crushed (But Still Whole)
2 Tablespoons Butter or Olive Oil
Sprig of Fresh Rosemary
Dash of Worcestershire Sauce
1/4 Teaspoon Pepper

In sauce pan, sauté garlic in butter or oil over medium heat. Add wine and remaining ingredients. Heat to bubbling, stirring frequently. Simmer until reduced to about 3/4 of a cup, about 45 minutes to an hour. Remove rosemary and garlic before using sauce on pizza.

The Early Birds Catch a Stone

If you are only going to barbeque pizzas a time or two, then you can make do with the thin pizza stones sold in stores like Target or Bed Bath and Beyond. However, these tend to crack rather quickly after macho cooks blast them with heat from flame throwing barbeques.

They are also thin and shatter if dropped on a concrete patio. In the early days, our pizza cooking was frequently preceded by stone puzzle assembly. We now use a stone that will break the patio and several toes if dropped. So much more sensible.

According to Greg and Rick, the absolutely best stone for barbequing pizzas is soapstone. It is worth noting that the stone these mad scientists prefer is the very same material used to make laboratory counters in research facilities around the world. This stone is completely impervious to abuse. It can take impossibly high temperatures and even the most corrosive chemical spills can't damage the surface.

Our macho cooks promptly confirmed these properties by attempting to ruin one of their brand new stones. They dropped a pizza on it. As with buttered toast and carpeting, the pizza landed topping side down. The guys were able to remove most of it, but the cheese decided to hang on.

They then cooked the stone until the stuck-on cheese turned to ash (about ten seconds or so) and then scraped everything off. Once the stone was successfully cleaned, they quickly declared the dropping of the pizza to be a deliberate test and certainly not the result of any horseplay at the barbeque.

To find these wonderful soapstones, the guys called up dozens of companies that make or install countertops to see if they had any remnants they would be willing to sell. Greg and Rick spent days on the phone before finding a company with the right size pieces.

Early Saturday morning they piled into the car and spent the whole day driving back and forth across Southern California to get their new stones. At least half of the driving was in the wrong direction because they did not confirm the location before leaving home. Macho drivers do not use maps or ask directions.

Never underestimate the power of pity. The owner of the company felt so sorry for these two that even though he had waited for them past closing time, he still gave them the remnants for free, instead of charging them the price originally quoted. The guys arrived home, having spent more in gas than it would have cost to buy from a local supplier, and having wasted an entire day to boot.

The dinner they stopped to eat in celebration of their success brings the total cost per foot up to something the military would pay. The time and gas is not something these two will ever mention when telling of their triumph of acquiring "free" pizza stones. They do not understand why their wives don't appreciate how frugal they are.

Our pizza stone is enormous. It is more than an inch thick, over a foot wide and almost three feet long. It probably weighs over seventy pounds, and takes two people to lift it. To get it heated through takes at least half an hour. But once it is hot a pizza will cook almost instantaneously.

How do you know when the stone is hot enough to cook? Remember the macho cook's tendency to accumulate every possible gadget imaginable? Judging the heat of a pizza stone cannot be done by such outdated methods as holding a hand above it or seeing if a drop of water will dance and boil on the surface. Macho cooks need a high-tech tool for taking temperature readings.

A pizza stone absolutely must be heated to a cooking temperature of exactly 450 degrees. This, the macho cooks declare, is the precise temperature needed to achieve Nirvana: the perfect pizza. The fact that most other chefs have cooked pizzas perfectly well at a wide range of other temperatures is stuff and nonsense. Wives are not to reference any recipes or cooking shows that dispute the 450 degree decree!

It is a well known fact that too hot a stone will result in a crust that is done while the toppings are still almost raw. And of course the reverse is also true – a stone below 400 is not hot enough to cook the crust before the pizza toppings become overcooked. This result is achieved by opening the barbeque too often to check on the pizzas or measure the temperature of the stone.

You do need to open a barbeque once during cooking to rotate the pizza so that it cooks evenly. Unfortunately, macho cooks have difficulty resisting the impulse to rotate pizzas incessantly, spinning them as though they were being roasted on a spit. This inevitably cools the barbeque and pizza stone to the point where cooking effectively stops.

I can still remember the days before barbeque thermometers. The caveman style of grilling, where the heat of the barbeque was adjusted based on how quickly the food itself was cooking. After the invention of the barbeque thermometer, cooks began relying on this gadget and disregarding the appearance of the food. A blackened hot dog was not burned because the barbeque had never exceeded 300 degrees. That blood red burger is definitely completely cooked, the barbeque was over 400 degrees.

UH... NO, NOTHING IS WRONG. IM JUST CHECKING THE TEMPERATURE INSIDE THE ICE CHEST.

Fortunately for our bellies, if not for our wallets, the march of technology continues. No longer is it necessary to use just a simple thermometer to judge the cooking readiness of a barbeque. With the development of the "High-Tech Infrared Temperature Sensor Gun with Laser Sight" you too can measure the temperature of a pizza stone and know to the hundredth of a degree exactly how hot it is. (And look like Clint Eastwood while you are doing so.)

Readings can be taken both in Celsius or Fahrenheit just to add a little extra confusion. If the temperature reads 449.99 you can turn the burners up and if the temperature rises to 450.01 you can turn the burners down again. With a response time of 500 milliseconds the temperature readings will change faster than you can turn the knobs on the barbeque.

This expensive little gadget is one of the most impressive tools in Greg's barbequing arsenal and the guys have lots of fun with it. It shines a little red dot on wherever you are measuring temperature and Greg thinks it is funny to watch the cat chase the dot across the patio. I am so afraid that one day I am going to have to explain to our vet how the cat came to jump up on a hot pizza stone.

Once it is hot, a pizza stone will hold heat for many, many hours. Thick pizza stones cool at about the same rate as glaciers melt. We know this. We have owned a thick pizza stone for a long time now. The pizza stone cannot be removed from the barbeque on the same night as it was used.

A person should not attempt to pick up a stone with bare hands without first verifying that it is cool enough to touch. And we have the technology to check this without touching the stone. Why is a tool that is indispensable when cooking and used frequently for non-cooking temperature sensing (how hot is the patio ceiling?) not allowed to be used when the barbeque is off?

Greg's reasons never make sense. "You are not a macho cook, therefore you should not use macho cooking tools." (Translation: It's mine and I don't want to share.) "The gun has already been cleaned and put away." (Taking it out of a drawer and pointing it at the stone will require tremendous effort and copious clean up.) Or my personal favorite: "It isn't necessary." Said just before my macho cook grabs the pizza stone with both hands and screams in pain.

Pizza Cooking

Prewarm the pizza stone in the barbeque to about 450 degrees before rolling out dough. This will take about half an hour or so for thick soapstones, less for the thin ceramic stones.

If the dough sits on the peel too long before cooking it swallows up the corn meal that keeps it from sticking. Strangely enough this results in the pizza dough becoming stuck to the peel. Removing an uncooked pizza complete with toppings is probably how calzones were invented. This is why I usually wait until the barbeque has been on for at least fifteen minutes before starting pizza construction.

If you decide to cook your pizzas in a regular oven, you will probably need a longer preheating time. (Why did you buy a book on barbequing pizzas if you intended to use an oven? Seems a bit crazy. Oh, wait crazy is the group most likely to buy a book about what not to do when making pizzas. Carry on then, glad to have you aboard.)

Barbeque burners when turned up can kick out a lot more heat than most oven burners. Our pizza stone is too large to fit in our oven, but thanks to Barbara's baking group, I can tell you that it took an hour at 500 degrees to get the stone hot enough to cook in the short times listed for these recipes. Cooking times for the first pizzas they made were considerably longer than listed.

The barbeque should be set to maintain the pizza stone at a temperature somewhere between 400 and 500 degrees, depending on the thickness of the crust, how many toppings you have piled on and how well heat circulates in the barbeque. Each barbeque will cook differently, so you will have to adjust temperatures and times to fit your particular barbecue.

If the crust is cooking faster than the toppings try turning down the burner under the center of the pizza stone and increase the heat on the burners at the sides to increase the heat circulating up above the pizza. You can use a sensor gun that reads the temperature of the pizza stone. On sale, they are only twenty or thirty dollars.

When you are ready to start cooking pizzas, flatten a ball of pizza dough into a rough circle by patting it with floured hands. Then use a rolling pin to roll the dough out on a well floured surface. You can toss the dough up in the air if you want a real mess. When tossing, the extra flour leaves the dough at high velocity. Brian did this very well, he would flour everything within a five foot radius.

Once the dough is a reasonable size and shape, (triangles taste just as good as circles) gently shake off the extra flour and put it on a pizza peel that has been sprinkled with a liberal amount of corn meal (a tablespoon or two). Assemble the pizza on the peel.

First spread sauce on the dough. Be creative, just about any sauce can be used if it sounds good to you. We have tried marinara, alfredo, pesto, ranch dressing, mustard, barbeque sauce, enchilada sauce, steak sauce, honey and many others. You should not use a lot of sauce, a few tablespoons is usually enough to cover the entire dough surface. Too much sauce will make the pizza soggy and overwhelm the flavors of the toppings.

Next sprinkle the cheese on. Shredded mozzarella is the usual, but it is not the only cheese. Try different ones, mix a few together. Goat cheese, blue cheese, cheddar, Romano, and parmesan are just some of the ones we have tried and liked.

Third add your toppings. Meatballs, pepperoni, salami, salmon, chicken, onions, sundried tomatoes, bell peppers (yellow and orange are milder), capers, etc. The possibilities are endless. This is where the real fun of pizza making comes in. When you create something delicious and unique like steak with wine reduction sauce, it is so wonderful to share it.

One warning I have is that sweet toppings can ruin pizza stones – the sugars stick and caramelize on the stone. But pears, dried cranberries, nuts and goat cheese over a honey sauce are well worth the risk. If you suspect a pizza may be at risk of bubbling sauce or toppings onto the stone, you can put it on a pizza pan and cook it in the pan on the stone.

After putting toppings on, add a little more cheese; parmesan or Romano perhaps. Thin sliced toppings like pepperoni or salami tend to dry out and over cook, so put quite a bit of cheese over those toppings.

With the pizza stone at 450 degrees, a pizza will take 6 or 7 minutes to cook. At 500 degrees it will take 4 to 5 minutes. Pizzas should be turned a time or two in the middle of cooking to get them to cook evenly. This is what the metal peel is for. It slides easily under a cooking pizza and lets you rotate it a ¼ turn without too much trouble.

You will also use the metal peel to lift the pizza off the stone when it is done. HOWEVER do NOT use the metal peel to carry a pizza. Transfer the pizza to a wood peel before taking a single step away from the barbeque. Remember the pizza slides very easily on the metal peel. It slides right off as soon as you try to walk with it. A fact our dogs are well aware of. They know you only have to cause the cook to dodge once to get an entire pizza to hit the ground.

The following recipes should be used as a starting point. When we make pizzas we don't measure any of the toppings. We just pile them on until the pizza looks about right. Expect to adjust all these recipes to your own taste. If you love cheesy pizza then add more cheese. Hate onions? Leave them off. Experiment and enjoy!

Recipes are like Italian traffic laws, just vague suggestions on how to proceed. Any part of a recipe or traffic sign that is distasteful or inconvenient can be safely ignored. Just plow ahead at full speed and make rude hand gestures at anyone who complains.

I expect and even encourage you to make copious adjustments to my recipes. Change any, or even all of the ingredients and the amounts. Cook in a different way at a completely random temperature for whatever time you prefer. If the recipe comes out well take all the credit, after all you made changes so the recipe doesn't really count.

However if the experiment is a failure then blame my recipe, after all you followed it quite closely. I've been blamed for a lot of bad pizzas in my time, one more or less isn't going to make much of a difference. Just don't blame me for sauerkraut, I've warned you repeatedly against sauerkraut and take absolutely no responsibility if it has been used.

Traditional Pizza Recipes

These recipes are what we normally think of when pizza is mentioned. The favorites that everyone loves. You can add your own special touch by using fresh ingredients like homegrown vegetables, or homemade sauces.

Barbeque Chicken Pizza

Our favorite takeout salad is the Chopped BBQ Chicken Salad from Red's Barbecue. They use a dill ranch dressing and then a drizzle of barbecue sauce too. This pizza was inspired by their salad and we use Red's dressing and barbecue sauce on our version.

1 White Pizza Dough
1 Tablespoon Cornmeal
3 Tablespoons Ranch Dressing
1 Cup Shredded Mozzarella
4 Ounces Grilled chicken, Diced
1/4 Cup Red Onions, Sliced or Chopped
1/4 Cup Red and Yellow Peppers, Chopped
2 Tablespoons Barbeque Sauce

This pizza is a family favorite and also a source of contention. Some family members feel the pizza should not have peppers on it. I like the peppers, and since I wrote the recipe down, it has peppers in it. You will have to try it both ways and come to your own decision on peppers.

Preheat pizza stone at 450 degrees. Roll out the dough on a floured board. Sprinkle cornmeal on peel. Gently shake extra flour off dough and put on peel.

Spread ranch dressing on dough. Sprinkle on most of the cheese. Arrange chicken, peppers and onions on pizza. Sprinkle remaining cheese over the top. Drizzle with barbeque sauce.

Cook on 450 degree pizza stone until dough is done, about 6 minutes.

Pair with Vinemark Cellars Primitivo, a robust, fruity red. The Vinemark label is brand spanking new (launched in the Spring of 2013). Our friends, Mark and Julie Wasserman, have been making yummy wines for many, many years. It is so much fun to see them finally living their dream! You go guys! Their website is www.vinemarkcellars.com.

Buffalo Chicken Pizza

Some like it hot! (Marilyn, of course.) This pizza is for those of you who like more spice or zing than the Barbeque Chicken Pizza.

1 Beer Pizza Dough
1 Tablespoon Cornmeal
4 Tablespoons Ranch Dressing
1 Cup Shredded Mozzarella
1 Cup Grilled Chicken, Cut in Small Pieces
1/2 Cup French Fried Onions
1/4 Cup Grated Romano Cheese
2 Tablespoons Hot Sauce or Frank's Buffalo Wing Sauce

Preheat pizza stone to at least 450 degrees. Roll out the dough on a floured board. Sprinkle cornmeal on peel. Gently shake extra flour off dough and put on peel.

Spread ranch dressing on dough. Sprinkle mozzarella on dough. Arrange chicken and onions over the top. Sprinkle romano on pizza. Drizzle hot sauce on top.

Cook on 450 degree pizza stone until dough is done and cheese is melted, about 6 minutes.

Pair with Dark Star Left Turn, a blend of Zinfandel, Syrah, and Mourvedre. A smooth, balanced, but in your face wine that can stand up to a buffalo. Dark Star is a small family winery with delicious wines at reasonable prices.

The owners, Norm and Susan Benson are friendly, down to earth people. Norm focuses on producing their premium hand crafted red wines. You'll usually find Susan in the tasting room and most times their two boxer pups as well. Their website is www.darkstarcellars.com.

Deli Pizza

For those of us who remember the old comic strip, this is the kind of pizza Dagwood would make. Just pile on every kind of lunch meat you can get your hands on.

1 Whole Wheat Pizza Dough
1 Tablespoon Cornmeal
3 Tablespoons Yellow Mustard
1 1/2 Cups Shredded Four Cheese Blend
2 Slices of Pastrami, Cut in Small Pieces
2 Slices of Roast Beef or Corned Beef, Cut in Small Pieces
6 Slices of Salami
8 Slices of Pepperoni
1/4 Cup Grated Parmesan

Preheat pizza stone at 450 degrees. Roll out the dough on a floured board. Sprinkle cornmeal on peel. Gently shake extra flour off dough and put on peel.

Spread mustard on dough. Sprinkle cheese blend on pizza. Arrange deli meats on pizza. Sprinkle parmesan cheese over the top.

Cook on 450 degree pizza stone until dough is done, about 6 minutes.

Pair with Edward Sellers Vertigo, a Grenache wine enhanced with Syrah and smoky Mourvèdre. This elegant wine with its berry aromas and lingering finish is just right for a meat heavy pizza. Edward Sellers is passionate about the art of wine making. Website: www.edwardsellers.com.

Enchilada Pizza

Living in Southern California, we eat a lot of Mexican food. So naturally we tried putting it on pizza and found it was quite tasty!

1 Wheat Pizza Dough
1 Tablespoon Cornmeal
5 Tablespoons Enchilada Sauce
1 Cup Shredded Four Cheese Mexican Blend
4 Ounces Grilled Chicken, Cut in Chunks
1 Tablespoon Jalapeno Peppers, Diced
2 Tablespoons Olives, Sliced
1/4 Cup Onions, Sliced

Fresh Cilantro, Chopped
1 Teaspoon Hot Sauce

Preheat pizza stone to at least 450 degrees. Roll out the dough on a floured board. Sprinkle cornmeal on peel. Gently shake extra flour off dough and put on peel.

Spread the enchilada sauce on dough. Sprinkle on most of the cheese. Arrange chicken, peppers, olives and onions on pizza. Sprinkle cilantro and remaining cheese over the top. Drizzle with hot sauce.

Cook on 450 degree pizza stone until dough is done, about 6 minutes.

Pair with Firestone Walker DBA (double barrel ale), a gold medal winner of extraordinary character and complexity. Being right smack in the middle of wine country, Firestone uses toasted American oak barrels for fermenting. This gives their ale unique hints of smoke and vanilla. Their website is www.firestonebeer.com.

Ham and Pineapple Pizza

When the kids were little this was my go to meal, the favorite that everyone would eat. I did have to make a rule that they had to eat everything, not just the pineapple.

1 White Pizza Dough
1 Tablespoon Cornmeal
4 Tablespoons Pizza (recipe in sauce section) or Marinara Sauce
1 Cup Mozzarella
6 Slices Ham or Canadian Bacon, Chopped
1/2 Cup Pineapple Cut in Small Chunks (If Using Frozen Defrost and Drain First, If Canned Drain Well)
1 Tablespoon Grated Parmesan or Romano Cheese

Preheat pizza stone to at least 450 degrees. Roll out the dough on a floured board. Sprinkle cornmeal on peel. Gently shake extra flour off dough and put on peel.

Spread sauce on dough. Sprinkle mozzarella on top. Arrange ham and pineapple on pizza. Sprinkle with grated parmesan cheese.

Cook on 450 degree pizza stone until dough is done and cheese is melted, about 6 minutes.

Pair with Sculpterra Viognier, a crisp white wine bursting with ripe melon and sweet peach flavors. Sculpterra's winemaker, Paul Frankel, is one of the nicest young men we know. He not only wins lots of impressive awards with his wines, he also loves to share his expertise. He and Greg have spent countless hours discussing grape growing, yeasts, barrels and so many other boring details of winemaking. (Over glasses and glasses of wine, of course.)

Thankfully, the winery boasts a beautiful sculpture garden, where the poodles and I can wander instead of listening to them. If you visit, bring a picnic and relax at one of the tables in the garden. Paul's website is www.sculpterra.com.

Meat Lovers Pizza

This pizza will quickly satisfy a bunch of hungry guys.

1 Herb Pizza Dough
1 Tablespoon Cornmeal
5 Tablespoons Pizza (recipe in sauce section) or Marinara Sauce
1 Cup Shredded Mozzarella
1 Link of Italian Sausage, Cooked and Crumbled
4 Meatballs, Sliced in Thirds
1 Ounce Sliced Pepperoni (About 8 Slices)
1/4 Cup Sliced Mushrooms
1 Tablespoon Fresh Basil, Chopped

Preheat pizza stone at 450 degrees. Roll out the dough on a floured board. Sprinkle cornmeal on peel. Gently shake extra flour off dough and put on peel.

Spread sauce on dough. Sprinkle most of cheese over sauce. Arrange sausage, meatballs, pepperoni, mushrooms and basil on pizza. Sprinkle the rest of the cheese over the top.

Cook on 450 degree pizza stone until dough is done and cheese is melted, about 4 minutes.

Pair with Petite Sirah, an inky wine with black pepper, plum and blackberry flavors. Opolo is a winery with great people, great food, and award winning wines. Opolo's owners, Dave and Rick, are friendly and fun. They hold lots of events during the year, our favorite being their summer wine blending party. Website: Opolo.com.

Meatball Pizza

This is one of my favorites, a pizza I make the main part of my meal.

1 Herb Pizza Dough
1 Tablespoon Cornmeal
4 Tablespoons Pizza (recipe in sauce section) or Marinara Sauce
1 Cup Shredded Mozzarella
6 Meatballs, Sliced in Thirds

1/2 Cup Chopped Onions
1/2 Cup Chopped Tomatoes
1/4 Cup Chopped Bell Peppers

Preheat pizza stone at 450 degrees. Roll out the dough on a floured board. Sprinkle cornmeal on peel. Gently shake extra flour off dough and put on peel.

Spread sauce on dough. Sprinkle most of cheese over sauce. Arrange meatballs, onions, tomatoes and peppers on pizza. Sprinkle the rest of the cheese over the top.

Cook on 450 degree pizza stone until dough is done and cheese is melted, about 6 minutes.

Pair with Eberle Zinfandel, a deep colored wine with jammy berry flavors and a peppery finish. Eberle is one of the wineries that built Paso Robles into the premier wine region it is today. It has been around forever and sits right out on Highway 46.

Gary Eberle is a big friendly bear of a man who cooks some great barbeque. He has a couple of gorgeous standard poodles that wander about the tasting room most days. Their website is www.eberlewinery.com.

Pepperoni Pizza

Pepperoni is a must have when making pizzas. The only question is whether to make it a straight pepperoni or whether to add extra touches. The thin pepperoni slices dry out when cooking, to avoid this cover them with a thin layer of cheese.

1 Herb Pizza Dough
1 Tablespoon Cornmeal
4 Tablespoons Pizza (recipe in sauce section) or Marinara Sauce
1 Cup Shredded Mozzarella
2 Ounces Sliced Pepperoni (about 15 slices)
Variations Add 1 or More:
1/2 Cup Chopped Onions
1/2 Cup Sliced Mushrooms
2 Ounces Sliced Black Olives

Preheat pizza stone at 450 degrees. Roll out the dough on a floured board. Sprinkle cornmeal on peel. Gently shake extra flour off dough and put on peel.

Spread sauce on dough. Sprinkle most of cheese over sauce. Arrange pepperoni and any variations on pizza. Sprinkle the rest of the cheese over the top.

Cook on 450 degree pizza stone until dough is done and cheese is melted, about 6 minutes.

Pair with Dark Star's signature wine, Ricordati (always remember), a Bordeaux style blend. Bold and fruity, this deep dark wine has won 18 Gold Medals and Best In Class at International Wine Competitions. Dark Star is a small family winery with delicious wines at reasonable prices.

The owners, Norm and Susan Benson are friendly, down to earth people. Norm focuses on producing their premium hand crafted red wines. You'll usually find Susan in the tasting room and most times their two boxer pups as well. Their website is www.darkstarcellars.com.

Pulled Pork Pizza

Here we have one of Greg's favorite pizzas. It comes out differently depending on who makes it. Some of us use the sweet barbeque sauce, some like the hot, spicy sauce and those who can't decide use a mixture of both.

1 White Pizza Dough
1 Tablespoon Cornmeal
5 Tablespoons Barbeque Sauce
1 Cup Shredded Four Cheese Blend
4 Ounces Pulled Pork, Shredded
1/4 Cup Mini Peppers, Diced
1/4 Cup Red Onions, Sliced or Chopped

Preheat pizza stone at 450 degrees. Roll out the dough on a floured board. Sprinkle cornmeal on peel. Gently shake extra flour off dough and put on peel.

Spread sauce on dough. Sprinkle on most of the cheese. Arrange pulled pork, peppers and onions on pizza. Sprinkle remaining cheese over the top.

Cook on a 450 degree pizza stone until the dough is done, about 6 minutes.

Pair with Jada's Jersey Girl, a sweet, smoky Syrah. Jada Vineyard and Winery is on the West Side of Paso Robles, where the mineral soils and cooling ocean air combine to make one of the best grape growing areas in the world. (Howls of outrage will not alter my opinion. But all you foreign wine producers are welcome to send me samples to try and change my mind.) Jada's website is www.jadavineyard.com.

Tri Tip Pizza

Tri tip is a barbequing staple, so if you are barbequing pizzas you have to try it sometime. Just think of it as a giant open faced tri tip sandwich.

1 Herb Pizza Dough
1 Tablespoon Cornmeal
3 Tablespoons Barbeque Sauce
1 Cup Shredded White Cheddar
4 Ounces Tri Tip, thinly sliced
1/2 Cup French Fried Onions
1 Tablespoon Minced Garlic

Preheat pizza stone at 450 degrees. Roll out the dough on a floured board. Sprinkle cornmeal on peel. Gently shake extra flour off dough and put on peel.

Spread barbeque sauce on dough. Sprinkle on most of the cheese. Arrange tri tip and onions on pizza. Sprinkle garlic and remaining cheese over the top.

Cook on 450 degree pizza stone until dough is done, about 6 minutes.

Pair with Tolosa Syrah, a bright ruby wine with an aroma of plums, violets, and a hint of leather. Tolosa is in the Edna Valley, a forty five minute drive south of Paso Robles. Their tasting room has big windows looking down into the winery and all the gleaming tanks of wine in the making. Website: www.tolosawinery.com.

Winey Cooks

Every so often you will come across one of those signs that says "I love cooking with wine, sometimes I even put it in the food." This is supposed to be a joke. Greg and Rick adhere to it as though it were a law. It can't be an unwritten rule, they've got it in writing on a decorative sign.

Should some catastrophic disaster occur that wipes out their wine collections then they will concede that it is possible to make pizza without wine. But then you had better have some really good beer to put in the cook instead. Remember macho cooks are an alcohol fueled species.

Wine consumption while cooking creates a serious hazard that should be mentioned. The cook may attempt to wave the smoke out of his face while holding a glass of wine. Or just randomly wave his arms to make a point or get someone's attention. The wine that splashes on the cooking pizzas will usually not be a problem. The heat and alcohol will kill any germs and wine usually goes well with just about any pizza topping.

However, the wine that splashes on the guests standing near the barbeque can be a problem. Good friends usually know better than to wear something that could be ruined. New friends should be warned of the danger and offered the use of a raincoat if they insist on standing near the cook. (I have never actually had to produce a raincoat, most people are either sensible enough to just stand clear or are drunk enough that they won't remember whether they spilt the wine themselves or not.)

For those who have not heard the term before, a pizza peel is the flat, shovel shaped tool with a long handle. The wide part is large enough to hold an entire pizza and the handle is long enough to keep your hands out of the barbeque when moving pizzas on or off the grill. It quickly became clear during the experimentation process that pizza peels were necessary if we wanted to reduce the consumption of first aid materials.

Greg naturally bought every type of pizza peel available locally. These are "tools." Have you ever looked in a guy's tool box? There are fourteen of every tool. They vary almost imperceptively in size and shape. There is one of each tool that is used every time. The other thirteen are just to impress their buddies. The same principle applies to barbequing tools.

So, we have short, fat peels and long, skinny peels. We have wood peels and metal peels. We have peels in a yellowish wood and peels in brown wood. We have thick peels and thin peels. We have long handled peels and short handled peels. And all of Greg's barbequing buddies are suitably impressed.

Pizza peels are used for assembling pizzas, turning them on the barbeque or carrying them to the table. You can't cut and serve pizzas on them, it will ruin the surface and make dough much more likely to stick.

We have found that uncooked pizza dough sticks to any kind of peel if left on the peel for very long. So, we learned to never assemble a pizza on a peel unless we would be able to put it onto the grill immediately after assembling. We also learned to use several tablespoons of corn meal on the peel to help prevent sticking. Overall, the wood peels gave less problems with sticking than the metal peels.

Cooked pizza, on the other hand, does NOT stick to peels. It slides off quite easily, especially when carried by someone whose wine consumption would get them elected in Italy or arrested if out in public.

Once a cook reaches the staggering drunk stage it is time to stop barbequing pizzas. I say this not so much out of concern for the cook (who could light up like a tiki torch at any moment), but rather out of concern for the pizzas. Nothing consumable is going to make it to the table after the cook has had two too many.

One bit of warning: even a halfway sober cook will drop pizzas off of metal peels. We have found the metal peels to be very useful for turning pizzas while on the grill – and absolutely nothing else.

You will need a table for the cook to put his peels on. Unfortunately, this can create a hazard. The cook will invariably also use the table for putting his wine glass on. With their long handles and wide shape, peels are uniquely talented at knocking wine glasses off of tables.

This disaster requires the lightening reflexes of an over-caffeinated mongoose, exactly the opposite of the reflexes that your drunk cook would have at this point. Since guests like to stand near the cook, now you have a guest who not only has wine in their shoe, but broken glass as well. Guests tend to lift the injured foot high in the air, becoming unsteady in the process. They will normally brace a hand on the nearest object to maintain their balance.

You must quickly insert something between the injured guest and the barbeque if you do not want to add third degree burns to the injuries. (Helpful Tip: Invite the paramedics to stay for pizza after treating injured guests. This allows them to get familiar with the barbeque location and will make future visits much more efficient.)

You would think that with all the pizza and wine Greg and Rick consume, and all the splashes that happened while experimenting, that these Edison's of barbequed pizzas had the idea for a wine sauce themselves. Nope. The thought never even crossed their minds.

Rick saw a pizza with wine sauce on a cooking show. Of course, macho cooks do not watch cooking shows, he claims to have just been flipping channels. Be that as it may, the cooking show finally shed some light on the relationship between pizza and wine. Rick did not record the cooking show. He did not write the recipe down. He thinks he remembers what wine was used, but very little else.

The lack of a recipe or even a vague idea of what they were attempting did not slow the experimenters down. These are macho cooks, they don't need no stinking directions!

They poured a bottle of wine into a sauce pan with whatever spices were nearby and cooked it down to a paste. They did not use the same wine Rick had seen on the show. They guessed at the amount of spicing, how much heat to use and how long to cook it.

This took a few hours and three bottles of wine. (Two were poured into the cooks.) They sampled the sauce frequently and debated the spicing and cooking procedures incessantly. Their bickering drove Marianne and me out of the kitchen. When they had just enough sauce left in the pan for one pizza, they finally stopped cooking.

They sautéed some mushrooms and onions with some chopped up leftover carne asada and put it on the dough. Without sauce or cheese. After this pizza was cooked they drizzled the wine reduction sauce over the pizza.

It did not look much like a pizza. However it was delicious and has since been made with many variations, including adding blue cheese or mozzarella. The sauce usually works best drizzled after cooking because otherwise it makes the crust too soggy.

Unusual and Exotic Pizza Recipes

As we were learning to barbeque pizzas we realized there were a lot more possibilities than just traditional pizzas. Experimenting with new ingredients and combinations is also a lot of fun!

Artichoke Pizza

This is the pizza that started it all. It has a wonderful mix of flavors with the artichoke hearts and sundried tomatoes. One caution is that this pizza can be a little on the salty side. We prefer to use a homemade pesto without any added salt. Most retail pestos add salt and with salt already in the artichokes, pepperoni and tomatoes that extra salt is just too much.

1 Beer Pizza Dough
1 Tablespoon Cornmeal
4 Tablespoons Pesto Sauce (recipe in sauce section)
1 Cup Shredded Mozzarella
2 Ounces (about 5 heart quarters) Marinated Artichoke Hearts, Drained and Chopped in Small Chunks
1 Ounce Pepperoni Slices (About 7), Chopped in Small Pieces
1 Ounce Sundried Tomatoes (About 7), Drained and Chopped in Small Chunks
2 Tablespoons Grated Parmesan or Romano Cheese

Preheat pizza stone at 450 degrees. Roll out the dough on a floured board. Sprinkle cornmeal on peel. Gently shake extra flour off dough and put on peel.

Spread pesto sauce on dough. Sprinkle cheese evenly on dough. Arrange artichoke hearts, pepperoni and tomatoes on pizza. Sprinkle grated cheese over the top.

Cook on 450 degree pizza stone until dough is done and cheese is melted, about 4 minutes.

Pair with Gelfand Vineyards' Zirah, a bold blend of dark, heavy Syrah and fruity Zinfandel. Len and Jan Gelfand are living their dreams with this small boutique winery. These wonderful people are passionate about their wines. Unfortunately, their outstanding wines are only made in small quantities. Their wine club gets first dibs and takes most of their production. Last I heard there was a waiting list to get into the club, but if you succeed in joining don't miss their annual party. Len's website is www.gelfandvineyards.com.

Bacon and Blue Burger Pizza

The most successful of our experiments were those that imitated a food we already liked. Greg took his favorite burger and made it into this delicious pizza.

1 Beer Pizza Dough
1 Tablespoon Cornmeal
5 Tablespoons Blue Cheese Dressing
1 Hamburger Pattie, Cooked and Crumbled
1/4 Cup Crumbled Bacon
1/2 Cup French Fried Onions
1/4 Cup Crumbled Blue Cheese

Preheat pizza stone at 450 degrees. Roll out the dough on a floured board. Sprinkle cornmeal on peel. Gently shake extra flour off dough and put on peel.

Spread dressing on dough. Arrange hamburger, bacon and onions on pizza. Sprinkle crumbled cheese over the top.

Cook on 450 degree pizza stone until dough is done, about 6 minutes.

Pair with Denner Vineyards' Zinfandel, which has flavors of berry, orange peel and pepper. The architecture of the Denner winery buildings is unique, and the view from the patio is lovely. If you want to visit you have to find a wine club member to go with and an appointment is necessary. But that means you'll be able to relax in an armchair by the fire while tasting instead of being sardined (this is a verb in my book, literally) at a bar. Their website is www.dennervineyards.com.

Bacon, Egg and Tomato Pizza

This pizza has its roots in Greg's childhood, when his mom would make bacon, egg and tomato sandwiches as a quick and easy dinner.

1 White Pizza Dough
1 Tablespoon Cornmeal
2 Tablespoons Mustard
1 Cup Shredded Cheddar Cheese
2 Eggs
1/2 Cup Cooked Bacon, Crumbled
1 Large Tomato, Sliced

Preheat pizza stone at 450 degrees. Scramble eggs and cook in frying pan.

Roll out the dough on a floured board. Sprinkle cornmeal on peel. Gently shake extra flour off dough and put on peel. Spread mustard on dough. Sprinkle half of cheese on dough. Arrange tomato slices on pizza. Sprinkle eggs, bacon and remaining cheese over the top.

Cook on 450 degree pizza stone until dough is done and cheese is melted, about 6 minutes.

Pair with Baileyana Winery's Blanc De Blanc Sparkling, a full-bodied dry white wine. Baileyana has sustainably farmed their wine grapes in the Edna Valley for over three decades. They produce wines of concentrated flavors and balanced acidity. Website: www.baileyana.com.

Carne Asada Pizza

This experiment started one night with some leftover carne asada. The first try wasn't quite right, but once we found the chimichurri sauce it was perfect.

1 Beer Pizza Dough
1 Tablespoon Cornmeal
3 Tablespoons Chimichurri Sauce (recipe in sauce section)
1 Cup Mexican Four Cheese Blend
4 Ounces of Carne Asada, Thinly Sliced
1/4 Cup Chopped Onion
1/4 Cup Cilantro, Chopped
1 Teaspoon Crushed Red Chili Peppers
1 Tablespoon Hot Sauce

Preheat pizza stone at 450 degrees. Roll out the dough on a floured board. Sprinkle cornmeal on peel. Gently shake extra flour off dough and put on peel.

Spread chimichurri sauce on dough. Sprinkle cheese on top. Arrange carne asada, onions and cilantro on pizza. Sprinkle hot sauce and red peppers over the top.

Cook on 450 degree pizza stone until dough is done, about 6 minutes.

Pair with Opolo's Tempranillo, a wine bursting with ripe berry and spice flavors. The long, rich finish complements the Carne Asada pizza perfectly. Opolo is a winery with great people, great food, and award winning wines. Opolo's owners, Dave and Rick, are friendly and fun. They hold lots of events during the year, our favorite being their summer wine blending party. Website: Opolo.com.

Jambalaya Pizza

This spicy, cajun recipe came from Yvonne, who makes an awesome jambalaya. This pizza is best cooked at lower temperatures (400 to 450), allowing a longer cooking time to heat up all the toppings. Like any good jambalaya, this hearty pizza has a little bit of everything.

1 White Pizza Dough
1 Tablespoon Cornmeal
4 Tablespoons Canned Diced Tomatoes
4 Tablespoons Tomato Sauce
1 Teaspoon Cajun Spice Blend (for sauce)
1 1/2 Cups Shredded Mozzarella
1 Link Cooked Louisiana Sausage, Diced
6 Medium Cooked Shrimp, Diced
1 Ounce Grilled Chicken Breast, Chopped
1/4 Teaspoon Cajun Spice Blend (for Vegetables)
1 Tablespoon Olive Oil
1/2 Cup Onion, Chopped
1/2 Cup Green Bell Pepper, Chopped
1/2 Cup Mushrooms, Sliced
1 Tablespoon Red Pepper Flakes

Sauté onion, bell pepper and mushrooms in olive oil with 1/4 teaspoon of cajun spice blend.

Preheat pizza stone to 425 degrees. Roll out the dough on a floured board. Sprinkle cornmeal on peel. Gently shake extra flour off dough and put on peel.

Mix tomatoes, tomato sauce and 1 teaspoon of cajun spice blend and spread on pizza. Sprinkle 1 cup of cheese over the top. Arrange sausage, shrimp and chicken on pizza. Sprinkle onion, peppers and mushrooms on top. Add the rest of the shredded mozzarella. Sprinkle red pepper flakes on top.

Cook on 425 degree pizza stone until dough is done, about 7 minutes.

Pair with Stone Brewing's Arrogant Bastard Ale, an aggressive beer that can stand up and fight with the spicy jambalaya pizza. This ale is full of passion, quality and depth. The tee shirt is fun too! Stone Brewing Company is a craft brewery that has been named "All-Time Top Brewery on Planet Earth" by Beer Advocate magazine twice! Their website is www.stonebrew.com.

New Delhi (Indian) Pizza

One night while experimenting, I handed Grace a jar of biryani paste I had found at a little Indian grocery in town. Grace's creation was an instant hit.

1 Herb Pizza Dough
1 Tablespoon Cornmeal
2 Tablespoons Tomato Sauce
2 Teaspoons Biryani Paste
3 Ounces Grilled Chicken Breast, Chopped
5 Garlic Cloves, Diced
2 Tablespoons Fresh Cilantro, minced
1/4 Cup Onion, Chopped
1 Cup Shredded Mozzarella

Preheat pizza stone to 450 degrees. Roll out the dough on a floured board. Sprinkle cornmeal on peel. Gently shake extra flour off dough and put on peel.

Mix tomato sauce and biryani paste and spread on pizza. Arrange chicken on pizza. Sprinkle garlic, cilantro and onion on top. Add the shredded mozzarella.

Cook on 450 degree pizza stone until dough is done, about 6 minutes.

Pair with Stone Brewing's IPA, an India Pale Ale, of course. The Stone India Pale Ale has a huge hop aroma, flavor and bitterness throughout. Stone Brewing Company is a craft brewery that has been named "All-Time Top Brewery on Planet Earth" by Beer Advocate magazine twice! Their website is www.stonebrew.com.

Pastrami Pizza

You either love the pastrami pizza or you hate it. There doesn't seem to be any middle ground with this one. Someone always asks to make one, and someone else always groans when they do. We use regular French's mustard as the sauce. For those of you who like their pizza a little fancier, you can substitute dijon or stone ground mustard.

1 White Pizza Dough
1 Tablespoon Cornmeal
2 1/2 Tablespoons Yellow Mustard
1 Cup Shredded Four Cheese Blend
4 to 5 Slices of Pastrami, Cut in Small Pieces
1/2 to 3/4 Cup (3 spears) Dill Pickles, Drained and Chopped

Preheat pizza stone at 450 degrees. Roll out the dough on a floured board. Sprinkle cornmeal on peel. Gently shake extra flour off dough and put on peel.

Spread mustard on dough. Sprinkle most of the cheese on pizza. Arrange pastrami and pickles on pizza. Sprinkle remaining cheese over the top.

Cook on 450 degree pizza stone until dough is done, about 6 minutes.

Pair with Brian Benson Cellars' Kandy Red, a wonderful blend of Zinfandel, Syrah, Grenache, and Mourvedre. This limited production wine comes in custom pinstriped collector bottles. Brian Benson, Norm and Susan's son, has his tasting room next door on the Dark Star property. His wines are getting wonderful reviews and are winning lots of awards. Although a third generation winemaker, Brian has his own distinct style and likes to age his wines obsessively long in the barrels. His website is www.brianbensoncellars.com.

Philly Cheesesteak Pizza

Yep, here is yet another sandwich turned into a pizza. Once we found mustard worked well as a sauce we went a bit crazy. (Hey! You have no proof on the timing.)

1 Herb Pizza Dough
1 Tablespoon Cornmeal
3 Tablespoons Mustard
1 Tablespoon Olive Oil
1/2 Cup Onions, Sliced
1/2 Cup Bell Peppers, Sliced
1/2 Teaspoon Black Pepper
8 to 10 Slices Provolone Cheese
4 to 6 Slices Roast Beef, Coarsely Chopped

Sauté onions and bell peppers in oil with black pepper. Preheat pizza stone at 450 degrees.

Roll out the dough on a floured board. Sprinkle cornmeal on peel. Gently shake extra flour off dough and put on peel.

Spread mustard on dough. Arrange slices of cheese on dough. Spread roast beef and sautéed peppers and onions over the top.

Cook on 450 degree pizza stone until dough is done and cheese is melted, about 6 minutes.

Pair with Sculpterra's Cabernet Sauvignon, a fruity, full-bodied wine with notes of cedar, toast and pepper. Sculpterra's winemaker, Paul Frankel, is one of the nicest young men we know. He not only wins lots of impressive awards with his wines, he also loves to share his expertise. He and Greg have spent countless hours discussing grape growing, yeasts, barrels and so many other boring details of winemaking. (Over glasses and glasses of wine, of course.)

Thankfully, the winery boasts a beautiful sculpture garden, where the poodles and I can wander instead of listening to them. If you visit, bring a picnic and relax at one of the tables in the garden. Paul's website is www.sculpterra.com.

Steak and Wine Pizza

This pizza is one of Rick's creations and a delicious one at that. Make the wine reduction sauce ahead of time, since it takes at least an hour to make. The wine reduction sauce will make the dough soggy, so it should be drizzled on right before cutting and eating.

1 Herb Pizza Dough
1 Tablespoon Cornmeal
1 Tablespoon Olive Oil
1/2 Cup Grilled Steak, Cut in Small Cubes
3/4 Cup Onions, Sliced
3/4 Cup Mushrooms (about 6 medium), Sliced
1 Tablespoon Butter or Olive Oil (for sautéing)
1/4 Cup Crumbled Blue Cheese
1/4 Cup Wine Reduction Sauce (recipe in sauce section)

Sauté onions and mushrooms in butter. Preheat pizza stone at 450 degrees.

Roll out the dough on a floured board. Sprinkle cornmeal on peel. Gently shake extra flour off dough and put on peel.

Brush dough with olive oil. Arrange steak, sautéed onions and mushrooms on pizza. Sprinkle crumbled blue cheese over the top.

Cook on 450 degree pizza stone until dough is done, about 5 minutes. Drizzle wine reduction sauce over the top after cooking. Slice and serve.

Pair with Starr Ranch Terrestris, a spicy, dark and distinctive Bordeaux blend of mostly Cabernet Franc. Starr Ranch is way out in the country, but worth the visit. It has a quiet, peaceful picnic area under the oak trees with plenty of tables and chairs. Judy Starr's vineyard produces high quality grapes that are prized by many wineries. She keeps a small amount of her best grapes for her own wines. Judy is a wonderful gal who likes to pair her wines with gourmet food. Make sure to grab her lemon bar recipe. Yum! Judy's website is www.starr-ranch.com.

Thai Chicken Pizza

We fell in love with Thai food on our vacation in Thailand. Our favorite dishes were those that mixed garlic and cilantro with the sweet and spicy sauces.

1 White Pizza Dough
1 Tablespoon Cornmeal
4 Tablespoons Thai Chili Sauce (Usually sweet and garlicky, this sauce is only mildly hot.)
1 Cup Shredded Mozzarella
4 Ounces Grilled Chicken, Cut in Chunks
1 Clove of Garlic, Diced
1/4 Cup Onions, Sliced
1/4 Cup Mini Peppers, Sliced

Fresh Cilantro, Chopped

1 Tablespoon Sriracha Sauce (Thai hot sauce that I have found in either the hot sauce or Asian sections of my local supermarket. This sauce has a lot of kick to it.)

Preheat pizza stone at 450 degrees. Roll out the dough on a floured board. Sprinkle cornmeal on peel. Gently shake extra flour off dough and put on peel.

Spread the chili sauce on dough. Sprinkle on most of the cheese. Arrange chicken, peppers and onions on pizza. Sprinkle cilantro, garlic, sriracha sauce and remaining cheese over the top.

Cook on 450 degree pizza stone until dough is done, about 6 minutes.

Pair with Turley's Juvenile, a Zinfandel with flavors of bitter chocolate, fruit and spice. Turley specializes in old vine Zinfandel and Petite Syrah wines. Their website is www.turleywinecellars.com.

Appearing Knowledgeable About Wine

Looking like a true wine connoisseur is fairly simple. First, pour only about a quarter to a third the amount of wine that your glass will hold. Hold the glass up to the light or a white background to see the color. Gently swirl the wine in the glass. (Now you understand why so little wine; if you poured too much you slosh on your shirt, or worse, the person next to you.)

Hold the wineglass under your nose with a serious expression on your face. Take a small sip and hold it in your mouth for a minute before swallowing. If you want to be really annoying, you can try a slurp and swish with the wine and claim the rude noise you are making is "volatizing the esters." (Practice several times before trying this in public, done wrong the wine comes out your nose and you look ridiculous.)

You can mumble a non-committal "hmmm" for added effect. Continue to drink the wine in small sips (unless you hate it, in which case you pour it in the dump bucket). You now look the part, that is all there is to it.

For those of you who want to sound like you know about wine there are a couple of quick and easy things to say. If you noticed an aroma or flavor in the wine that is usually the best comment. "I smell/taste fruit, pepper or berries etc..." Color is another easy thing to comment on. Wine should be bright and clear, not cloudy. Red wine is usually a purple red when it is young and becomes more brick colored (browner) as it ages. White wines typically start out pale and become darker and browner as they age as well. There are exceptions, but you are still safe just commenting on the shade without committing yourself to guessing the wine's age.

Still stuck for something to say? When all else fails read labels and signs, they tell you all sorts of stuff you can say. When driving past vineyards, Greg pointed out the different vines; Zinfandel, Syrah etc. When asked how he could tell, he said it was the shape of the vine, the way it was growing and the color of the leaves. At sixty miles per hour I couldn't see any difference between the vines. Then we passed a row with a little sign in front of it and Greg confessed "those little signs help a lot." If he hadn't been driving I'd have hit him!

You look like a wine expert, and you sound like a wine expert, so now you have a group of people who think you ARE a wine expert. How do you avoid revealing how little you really know? Ask the other people questions. What do you smell on the nose? What flavors are you tasting? What do you think of the color? Agree or use a non-committal "hmmm" from time to time.

After a few years of using these tactics you will have learned an awful lot from people who thought you knew more than they did. And voila, you are now a real wine expert.

Special Diets

Many of our family and friends follow special diets or have food allergies. I assume that if you or someone in your family has food allergies or a special diet, then you already know what should be done to accommodate their needs. These are just a few suggestions I have found helpful when friends join us for pizzas.

The most common food allergies are milk, peanuts, nuts, eggs, soy, fish, shellfish, citrus and wheat. We also have friends allergic to strawberries, chocolate and sesame. For most allergic people you simply have to avoid putting the problem food on the pizzas they will eat.

People with more difficult allergies will usually let you know before coming what their needs are. For instance some people are so allergic to peanuts that they cannot be in the same room with peanut products. Others are allergic to things that frequently hide in sauces and will need to read labels before eating. I am allergic to hazelnuts (which are sometimes called filberts) and therefore I read labels on baked goods and anything that is likely to use nuts.

We have quite a few vegetarians that join us for pizzas. Vegetarians vary quite a bit. So if you are inviting a vegetarian you should ask what their definition is. Some vegetarians just don't eat meats, but will eat seafood. For these friends, make sure to have plenty of vegetables and seafood ingredients. Check that the pizza sauces you will be using don't have sausage or other meats in them.

At the other extreme, vegans will eat no animal products at all. So you will need to make sure sauces have no eggs or cheese as well. You will also need to have some non-dairy shredded cheese for their pizzas. Most vegetarians are in the middle; they won't eat any meat or seafood, but eggs and cheese are fine.

Another special diet that is becoming more and more common is the gluten free diet. Since gluten is in wheat this diet requires special pizza dough. Making a good gluten free dough from scratch is a lot of work. Unless someone in your immediate family has a gluten intolerance, the recipes are too complex for the occasional pizza maker.

There are a few companies who make gluten free pizza dough mixes or flour mixes. You should be able to find a pizza dough mix in the baking section of your grocery store. From what I have read, a good gluten free flour mix has several different flours in it.

Wheat flour is frequently used in sauces and processed meats like pepperoni. So you will also need to check those labels to make sure they say "Gluten Free."

Both vegan and gluten free products are more easily found in newer grocery chains that focus on specialty foods and organic products. In my area Whole Foods, Trader Joes, and Sprouts carry more of these than Vons or Albertsons.

If you don't know where to look for specialty items, ask the guest where they shop for vegan or gluten free products. Or just ask that person to bring the item you are having trouble finding. Most people are just happy that you went to the trouble of thinking about what they would need.

Seafood and Vegetarian Pizza Recipes

These might be slightly healthier than some of our other recipes, but don't kid yourself. These are still pizzas, so mainly bread with lots of cheese. Our focus is on tasty and fun! Notice there is no attempt to measure nutritional value or calories. We don't want to know.

Arugula Flatbread

Flatbread is basically just really thin, crispy pizzas, sometimes in a rectangular shape. Use a third to half of the dough you would for a normal pizza. Go easy on the toppings, the thin crust won't support a normal pizza load. We've made these in an oblong octagon shape and cut them into squares. The actual rectangle shape we find to be geometrically impossible, as pizza dough is rather resistant to straight lines and simple geometric shapes, especially when rolling it out so thin.

1/2 Whole Wheat Pizza Dough
2 Tablespoons Cornmeal
2 Tablespoons Pesto Sauce (recipe in sauce section)
2 Ounces Buffalo Mozzarella, Sliced Very Thin

1 Handful of Arugula,
1/4 Cup Sliced Onions, Lightly Sautéed

Preheat pizza stone at 450 degrees. Roll out the dough as thin as you can get it on a floured board. Sprinkle cornmeal on pizza stone, and cook the dough on it at 450 degrees until the bottom of dough just begins to brown, about 1 or 2 minutes.

Sprinkle cornmeal on peel. Flip the dough over, putting the half cooked dough onto the peel cooked side up. Spread sauce thinly on dough. Arrange mozzarella slices on pizza. Sprinkle sautéed onions, and arugula over the top.

Cook a second time on a 450 degree pizza stone until dough is crisp, about 2 more minutes. These cook a lot faster than regular pizzas. Check them frequently.

Pair with Firestone Vineyard's Chardonnay, an Editors' Choice by Wine Enthusiast, this wine has aromas of apple and citrus with a hint of caramel. Firestone Vineyard is up on a mesa in the Santa Ynez Valley. Basically halfway between the Los Angeles area and Paso Robles, which makes it the perfect place to take a break from driving. Their website is www.firestonewine.com.

Cheese Pizza

Just because some grandchildren (we are not mentioning names here) won't eat anything but cheese pizza, that is no reason to make a Plain Jane version. The romano and parmesan cheeses help add flavor.

1 White Pizza Dough
1 Tablespoon Cornmeal
5 Tablespoons Pizza (recipe in sauce section) or Marinara Sauce
1 1/2 Cups Shredded Mozzarella

1/4 Cup Grated Romano Cheese
1/4 Cup Grated Parmesan Cheese

Preheat pizza stone to at least 450 degrees. Roll out the dough on a floured board. Sprinkle cornmeal on peel. Gently shake extra flour off dough and put on peel.

Spread sauce on dough. Sprinkle cheeses over the sauce.

Cook on 500 degree pizza stone until dough is done and cheese is melted, about 4 1/2 minutes.

Pair with Eberle's Sangiovese, a medium bodied wine with berry flavors, a hint of licorice and moderate tannins. Eberle is one of the wineries that built Paso Robles into the premier wine region it is today. It has been around forever and sits right out on Highway 46.

Gary Eberle is a big friendly bear of a man who cooks some great barbeque. He has a couple of gorgeous standard poodles that wander about the tasting room most days. Website: www.eberlewinery.com.

Chili Relleno Pizza

Because my recipe collection was rather lacking in vegetarian pizzas, I challenged all our friends to invent something new and different. Geri met my vegetarian challenge with this wonderful addition.

1 Beer Pizza Dough
1 Tablespoon Cornmeal
3 to 4 Tablespoons Double Roasted Salsa
2/3 Cup Fire Roasted Pasilla Chilies
1/4 Cup S&W Seasoned White Beans, drained
1 Cup Shredded Pepper Jack Cheese
1/4 Cup Cotija Cheese
1 Tablespoon Fresh Cilantro

Preheat pizza stone to at least 450 degrees. Roll out the dough on a floured board. Sprinkle cornmeal on peel. Gently shake extra flour off dough and put on peel.

Spread the salsa on the dough. Arrange the roasted chilies and beans on pizza. Sprinkle on the cotija cheese then the pepper jack. Arrange cilantro on top.

Cook on 450 degree pizza stone until dough is done, about 6 minutes.

Pair with Russian River Brewing Company's Pliny The Elder, a slightly bitter Double IPA (India Pale Ale). Russian River is owned by a couple of wine people who have gone over to the dark side. Which means they ruin perfectly good wine barrels by putting beer in them. (Did I mention I don't like beer?) However, Greg, Gareth and Brian all love their beers, especially the Plinys, so they must be doing something right. Their website is www.russianriverbrewing.com.

Margherita Pizza

Named after Queen Margherita of Italy, (and you thought I misspelled the name) this pizza is in the colors of the Italian flag; red, white and green.

1 Whole Wheat Pizza Dough
1 Tablespoon Cornmeal
3 Tablespoons Pizza (recipe in sauce section) or Marinara Sauce
4 Ounces Buffalo Mozzarella, Sliced
1 Large Beefsteak Tomato, Sliced
12 Fresh Basil Leaves, Chopped
1 Tablespoon Grated Parmesan or Romano Cheese

Preheat pizza stone at 450 degrees. Roll out the dough on a floured board. Sprinkle cornmeal on peel. Gently shake extra flour off dough and put on peel.

Spread sauce on dough. Arrange cheese and tomato slices on pizza. Sprinkle the chopped basil over the top. Sprinkle with grated cheese.

Cook on 450 degree pizza stone until dough is done and cheese is melted, about 6 minutes.

Pair with Opolo's Montagna-Mare, "mountain and sea" in honor of the Paso coastal mountains where grapes grow so well. This wine has flavors of berries, caramel, nuts and vanilla with a long finish.

Opolo is a winery with great people, great food, and award winning wines. Opolo's owners, Dave and Rick, are friendly and fun. They hold lots of events during the year, our favorite being their summer wine blending party. Website: Opolo.com.

Salad Pizza

A light and refreshing pizza. Now there is a phrase that you won't hear very often! Tangy arugula with sweet mandarin oranges and crunchy almond slices. Yum!

1 White Pizza Dough
1 Tablespoon Cornmeal
2 Tablespoons Orange Infused Olive Oil
1 Handful of Arugula Lettuce
1/4 Cup Sliced Almonds, lightly toasted

1/4 Cup Mandarin Oranges, Drained
1/2 Cup Crumbled Feta Cheese
1 Teaspoon Balsamic Vinegar or Peach Balsamic Vinegar

Lightly toast almond slices by spreading in a pan and putting under the broiler for a minute or two.

Preheat pizza stone at 450 degrees. Roll out the dough on a floured board. Sprinkle cornmeal on peel. Gently shake extra flour off dough and put on peel.

Brush dough with olive oil. Arrange arugula, almonds and oranges on pizza. Sprinkle feta cheese over the top.

Cook on 450 degree pizza stone until dough is done, about 6 minutes. Sprinkle vinegar over the pizza, slice and serve.

Pair with Tablas Creek's Patelin de Tablas Blanc, a crisp white wine with floral aromas. This Rhone blend is mostly Grenache Blanc, with Viognier, Roussanne, and Marsanne. Tablas Creek started with vines brought over from France. Their website is www.tablascreek.com.

Shrimp Pizza

Our oldest granddaughters make a special version for grandpa: they arrange the shrimp in a big heart shape on the pizza. Love those girls!

1 White Pizza Dough
1 Tablespoon Cornmeal
4 Tablespoons Pesto Sauce (recipe in sauce section)
1 Cup Shredded Mozzarella
15 Medium Size Cooked Shrimp
3 Marinated Artichoke Hearts, Drained and Chopped
1/4 Cup Onions, Sliced or Chopped

Preheat pizza stone at 450 degrees. Roll out the dough on a floured board. Sprinkle cornmeal on peel. Gently shake extra flour off dough and put on peel.

Spread sauce on dough. Sprinkle on most of the cheese. Arrange shrimp, artichokes and onions on pizza. Sprinkle remaining cheese over the top.

Cook on 450 degree pizza stone until dough is done, about 6 minutes.

Pair with Calcareous Winery's Twisted Sisters Chardonnay, a crisp fruity Chardonnay that is light on the oak. I love the Twisted Sisters name, bought the T-shirts because they were perfect for me and mine! Calcareous sits high on a hill in the coastal mountains on the west side of Paso. They have an absolutely spectacular view in all directions and lots of tables and chairs to enjoy it from. Their website is www.calcareous.com.

Smoked Salmon Pizza

This gourmet pizza we first tasted one summer in Italy. It was pouring down rain, so we ducked into the closest restaurant we could find and had a fantastic meal.

1 Herb Pizza Dough
1 Tablespoon Cornmeal
3 Tablespoons Alfredo Sauce (recipe in sauce section)
1 1/2 Cup Shredded Mozzarella
3 Ounces Smoked Salmon, Cut in Pieces
1 Tablespoon Capers
1/2 Teaspoon Fresh Dill, Finely Chopped

Preheat pizza stone at 450 degrees. Roll out the dough on a floured board. Sprinkle cornmeal on peel. Gently shake extra flour off dough and put on peel.

Spread sauce on dough. Sprinkle on most of the cheese. Arrange salmon and capers on pizza. Sprinkle dill and remaining cheese over the top.

Cook on 450 degree pizza stone until dough is done, about 6 minutes.

Pair with Sculpterra's Sauvignon Blanc, a crisp white wine with citrus and fruit flavors. Sculpterra's winemaker, Paul Frankel, is one of the nicest young men we know. He not only wins lots of impressive awards with his wines, he also loves to share his expertise. He and Greg have spent countless hours discussing grape growing, yeasts, barrels and so many other boring details of winemaking. (Over glasses and glasses of wine, of course.)

Thankfully, the winery boasts a beautiful sculpture garden, where the poodles and I can wander instead of listening to them. If you visit, bring a picnic and relax at one of the tables in the garden. Paul's website is www.sculpterra.com.

Thai Shrimp Pizza

Thai food is this wonderful fusion of Chinese and Indian food. Many dishes combine sweet and spicy as the Thai sweet chili sauce does.

1 Wheat Pizza Dough
1 Tablespoon Cornmeal
5 Tablespoons Thai Sweet Chili Sauce
1 Cup Shredded Mozzarella
12 Medium Shrimp, sliced in half
1 Teaspoon Chopped Garlic
1 Tablespoon Olive Oil
10 to 12 Sundried Tomatoes, Drained and Chopped into Small Pieces
1/4 Cup Onions, Chopped

Sauté shrimp and garlic with 2 Tablespoons of Thai chili sauce in olive oil. Preheat pizza stone at 450 degrees.

Roll out the dough on a floured board. Sprinkle cornmeal on peel. Gently shake extra flour off dough and put on peel.

Spread the rest of the chili sauce on dough. Sprinkle on most of the cheese. Arrange shrimp, sundried tomatoes and onions on pizza. Sprinkle remaining cheese over the top.

Cook on 450 degree pizza stone until dough is done, about 6 minutes.

Pair with Claiborne & Churchill's Dry Gewürztraminer, a fruity white with a spicy, floral nose. This is not the typical sweet Gewürztraminer, but dry, having very little residual sugar. They actually made this to be a dinner wine instead of a dessert wine. So I can drink this with dinner and still be (winecally) correct – instead of drinking an official dessert wine and getting laughed at. Claiborne & Churchill is in San Luis Obispo and their website is www.claibornechurchill.com.

Tostada Pizza

Robin and Mark came up with this delicious pizza recipe for my vegetarian challenge! Even I hadn't thought of using refried beans on pizza.

1 Beer Pizza Dough
1 Tablespoon Cornmeal
1 1/2 Cups Refried Beans
3 Tablespoons Hot Salsa
2 Tablespoons Chopped Green Onions
1/2 Cup Chopped Tomatoes
1 Tablespoon Fresh Cilantro
2 Cups Shredded Mexican Cheese Blend
1/2 Cup Chopped Lettuce
1/2 of an Avocado, Chopped

Preheat pizza stone to at least 450 degrees. Roll out the dough on a floured board. Sprinkle cornmeal on peel. Gently shake extra flour off dough and put on peel.

Spread the refried beans on the dough (heating the beans a little first makes this easier). Sprinkle on half of the cheese. Arrange salsa, tomatoes, cilantro and onions on pizza. Sprinkle remaining cheese over the top. Cook on 450 degree pizza stone until dough is done, about 6 minutes. Top with lettuce and avocado.

Pair with Stacked Stone Cellars' Gem, a bold, spicy red. Our wine tasting group was passing by Don's winery when someone mentioned how good his wines were. We were running early for our next appointment and so we turned the bus around (not easy on a narrow canyon road!) and dropped in. So glad we did! His website is www.stackedstone.com.

New Wine Drinkers

If you have friends just starting in wine, they will probably prefer light, sweet and fruity wines. Starting drinking wine is similar to starting drinking coffee. Most people start coffee with lots of sugar and milk, but as their palate matures they add less sweetening and become more particular about the flavor nuances.

My all time favorite sweet wine is Muscat Canelli. Muscat is inexpensive, so you can try lots of different ones without draining your bank account. Other white wines new wine drinkers might like would be Viognier and Gewurztraminer. These aren't quite as sweet as Muscat, but if done right they have a light pleasant flavor. However, there seems to be a lot more variation in how these grapes come out and the flavors will vary considerably between one winemaker and another.

Also look for wines with some residual sugar, wines that haven't been fermented all the way dry. California wines tend to be higher alcohol and/or sweeter than most other wines. California winemakers as a group tend to let grapes ripen on the vines longer than most other wine regions, probably due to our mild weather. Most other parts of the world run more of a risk of crop damage if they leave the grapes out too late in the season.

Since sugar in the grapes is converted to alcohol during fermentation, you would think the lower alcohol wines would all have residual sugar. However, the amount of sugar to start with is determined by the ripeness of the grapes. Lower alcohol can indicate the grapes were picked early and there may be bitter, vegetative undertones in the wine.

Chardonnay is not a sweet white, so it can take some getting used to for new wine drinkers. There is a strong flavor in the grape that is more noticeable if the grapes are fermented in stainless steel tanks. If you are going to serve Chardonnay to new wine drinkers then go for the buttery oaked Chardonnays, the oak tannins help hide the bitterness of the grape itself. (I have been asked to let you know that my opinion on Chardonnay is not necessarily shared by others in this house.)

Late harvest and dessert wines are also a good bet for new wine drinkers. They are extra sweet and since they are harvested when the grapes are all very ripe they avoid most of the vegetative flavors that take getting used to.

For red ports, I prefer Zinfandel ports to Cabernet ports. Many Cabs have vegetative flavors, which new wine drinkers usually don't like. Zinfandel, although a bold spicy grape, is much more likely to be drinkable for those of us with a sweet palate because it tends to have lots of fruit and berry flavors. Red ports should have some kind of chocolate served with them, because it makes such a wonderful combination.

Getting Our Just Desserts

A really good dessert pizza has been a goal of mine since we started experimenting. We've come up with some good ones and some that were not so good. We have tried using cookie dough instead of pizza dough by patting sugar cookie dough out flat on a pizza pan, adding toppings and barbequing it. This is NOT a dessert pizza. It is a large cookie that is either overcooked on the bottom or still raw on the top under the toppings or, as it was for us, both. As they say when demonstrating really stupid stunts; do not try this at home! It is awful.

If you don't want to make dessert dough, regular white pizza dough without any spicing works pretty well for dessert pizza. Plain dough with sprinkled cinnamon and sugar works better. One very important thing to remember is to go sparingly with sauces on dessert pizzas. Sugary or chocolaty sauces tend to make a gooey mess on pizza stones that is very hard to remove. Much worse than cheese.

I have been banned from putting fudge sauce on pizzas before cooking due to a minor little incident during one of our experiments. When making pizzas, you work with whatever is at hand. Someone had brought fruit salad as a side dish. I had a jar of fudge sauce. It sounded like a good combination.

I spread the fudge sauce on the dough. I did not heat the sauce first, so it went on rather thick and lumpy. Then I spooned the fruit salad over the top and drizzled a second chocolate sauce on top for good measure. The fruit salad was already a little runny before cooking.

Once on the grill, the fudge sauce melted and began spreading. The fruit produced a lot more juice. This mixture flowed off the dough in all directions. When the mixture met the pizza stone it hardened to something resembling burnt toffee.

After chipping the pizza loose it was found to be rather tasty, and suggestions for improvement were offered. However a second try was not allowed. Greg dumped the pizza stone in the trash and declared pizza making over for the night. (Thankfully this was before the purchase of his soapstone.)

I have never been permitted to put fudge sauce on an uncooked pizza since. The good news is that fudge, caramel and many other dessert sauces work well when added after the cooking is done. The same goes for whipped cream.

Dessert Pizza Recipes

Fruit is really good on dessert pizzas, BUT some fruits are too runny for pizza. Drain any fruit you are going to put on pizza really well, otherwise the crust will just be a soggy mess. You can also partially precook the dough to keep the dough from getting soggy or to keep from overcooking some of the toppings.

The sugar in the dessert dough has a tendency to burn and should be cooked on a cooler stone than regular dough. The cooler temperature also helps keep toppings from overcooking.

Banana Split Pizza

Colorful, yummy and fun! The only thing missing is the ice cream, which I suppose you could serve on the side if you wanted to.

1 Dessert Pizza Dough (Can substitute white dough with cinnamon sugar sprinkled on top)
1 Tablespoon Cornmeal
2 Tablespoons Honey or Caramel Sauce

1 or 2 Bananas, Sliced
12 Maraschino Cherry Halves, Drained
1 Tablespoon Chopped Macadamia Nuts
1/4 Cup Chocolate Chips
1/4 Cup Mozzarella
Whipped Cream

Preheat pizza stone at 400 degrees. Roll out the dough on floured board. Sprinkle cornmeal on peel. Gently shake extra flour off dough and put on peel.

Drizzle honey evenly over dough. (Do not spread, it will just pull the dough out of shape.) Arrange banana and cherry slices on dough. Sprinkle nuts, chocolate chips and mozzarella on top.

Cook on 400 degree pizza stone until dough is done, about 6 minutes. Serve with whipped cream (or ice cream if you dare).

Pair with Rotta Winery's Black Monukka. The nutty and caramel flavors in this cream sherry are perfect with the Banana Split Pizza! The Black Monukka grapes are aged in small oak barrels in the hot sun. Rotta Winery is the exclusive producer of this rare, sweet dessert wine. (Translation: This is the only winery I know of that is crazy enough to age a wine in the hot sun.)

Rotta Winery was one of the first wineries established in Paso Robles, and the only remaining family owned "original" winery in San Luis Obispo County. Website: www.rottawinery.com.

Chocolate Raspberry Pizza

Decadence. The name says it all. This pizza can be tricky. It gets soggy if too much port or too many raspberries are used. It also cooks best a little hotter than most pizzas, again to keep the crust from getting soggy.

1 Dessert Pizza Dough (Can substitute plain white dough with a little cinnamon sugar sprinkled on top.)

1 Tablespoon Cornmeal
3/4 Cup Shredded Mozzarella
1 Tablespoon Port Wine
3/4 Cup Fresh Raspberries
2 Tablespoons Sliced Almonds
1/2 Cup Chocolate Chips
2 Tablespoons Honey
Whipped Cream

Rinse raspberries and pat dry with paper towel. Mix port with honey. Soak raspberries in port mixture. Preheat pizza stone to 450 degrees. (If using plain dough 500 degrees will work.)

Roll out the dough on floured board. Sprinkle cornmeal on peel. Gently shake extra flour off dough and place it on the peel.

Sprinkle cheese on dough. Arrange raspberries, nuts and chocolate chips on top. Drizzle remaining port mixture over the pizza.

Cook on 450 degree pizza stone until dough is done, about 5 minutes. Serve with whipped cream.

Pair with PasoPort Wine Company's Ruby, a dark, mostly Zinfandel port with berry and licorice notes. PasoPort is a small, family-owned winery.

From the outside, the aging corrugated tin shack that serves as their tasting room looks like it has sat unchanged in the vineyard forever. A dirt road winds past it, leaving a coating of dust on the tin. But inside is a small, elegant bar with works of art on their bottles of heavenly dessert wine. Their website is www.pasoportwine.com.

Peach Pizza

Well, this is just peachy! (Sorry, can't resist a bad pun.)

1 Dessert Pizza Dough
1 Tablespoon Cornmeal
I Can Sliced Peaches, Drained
1/2 Cup Cream Cheese
1/2 Tsp Cinnamon

Preheat pizza stone at 400 degrees. Roll out the dough on floured board. Cook on 400 degree pizza stone for 2 minutes. Sprinkle cornmeal on peel. Place dough cooked side up on peel.

Soften cream cheese in microwave for about 20 seconds so it spreads easily. Spread cheese on the dough. Arrange peach slices on top. Sprinkle with cinnamon.

Cook on 400 degree pizza stone until dough is done, about another 4 minutes.

Pair with Eberle's Muscat Canelli, a light, fruity wine with just the right amount of sweetness. This is the best Muscat in California and I should know: I've tried just about all of them. Eberle is one of the wineries that built Paso Robles into the premier wine region it is today. It has been around forever and sits right out on Highway 46.

Gary Eberle is a big friendly bear of a man who cooks some great barbeque. He has a couple of gorgeous standard poodles that wander about the tasting room most days. Website: www.eberlewinery.com.

Pear Pizza

Tangy goat cheese with sweet fruit and crunchy almonds make a great pizza. Fresh pears are easy to work with because they don't make the pizza soggy. If you have to use canned pears then I suggest draining them well and perhaps cooking the crust a few minutes before topping.

1 Dessert Pizza Dough
1 Tablespoon Cornmeal
4 Tablespoons Honey or Caramel Sauce
1 Pear, Cored and Sliced Fairly Thin
2 Tablespoons Sliced Almonds
4 Tablespoons Dried Cranberries, Cherries or Figs
1 or 2 Ounces of Mascarpone or Goat Cheese
1 Tablespoon Cinnamon Sugar

Preheat pizza stone at 400 degrees. Roll out the dough on floured board. Sprinkle cornmeal on peel. Gently shake extra flour off dough and put on peel.

Drizzle half the honey or caramel sauce over dough. Arrange pear slices on dough. Dot with cheese. Add almonds and dried fruit. Sprinkle cinnamon sugar over the top.

Cook on 400 degree pizza stone until dough is done and pear slices are soft, about 6 minutes. Drizzle with rest of the honey or caramel sauce while still warm after cooking. (If you had put all the sauce on before cooking it would have run over the sides and made a sticky mess out of your pizza stone.)

Pair with Starr Ranch Sweet Chariot, a sweet blend of Muscat and Viognier that has flavors of apricot and pear. Starr Ranch is way out in the country, but worth the visit. It has a quiet, peaceful picnic area under the oak trees with plenty of tables and chairs.

Judy Starr's vineyard produces high quality grapes that are prized by many wineries. She keeps a small amount of her best grapes for her own wines. Judy is a wonderful gal who likes to pair her wines with gourmet food. Make sure to grab her lemon bar recipe. Yum! Judy's website is www.starr-ranch.com.

Pina Colada Pizza

Marianne created this pizza one night while we were hanging out on the patio. We were joking about having to run get another bottle of wine and saying it was a shame we couldn't combine alcohol with the pizza. She took that as a challenge and within a few minutes we were eating warm rum soaked pineapple.

1 White Pizza Dough
1 Tablespoon Cornmeal
1/2 Cup shredded Mozzarella
2 Tablespoons Rum
2 Tablespoons Brown Sugar
1 Cup Fresh Pineapple, in Small Chunks (Can Substitute Frozen or Canned, But Drain Well)
1/2 Cup Shredded Coconut
12 Maraschino Cherry Halves, Drained
2 Tablespoons Chopped Macadamia Nuts
2 Tablespoons Honey or Caramel Sauce
Whipped Cream

Soak pineapple and coconut in rum and brown sugar. Preheat pizza stone at 450 degrees.

Roll out the dough on floured board. Sprinkle cornmeal on peel. Gently shake extra flour off dough and put on peel. Sprinkle cheese on dough.

Arrange pineapple, coconut and cherries on cheese. Sprinkle with macadamia nuts. Mix honey with remaining rum and drizzle lightly over the top.

Cook on 450 degree pizza stone until dough is done, about 6 minutes. Serve with whipped cream.

Pair with (surely you guessed this already) a Pina Colada.

Pina Colada

Ice Cubes
1/2 Cup Rum (Most Recipes Use Light Rum, But Some Mix Light and Dark)
1/2 Cup Coconut Cream (or Coconut Milk Mixed With Condensed Milk)
1/4 Cup Heavy Cream or Whipping Cream (Optional)
1/4 Cup Pineapple (Crushed, Chunks or Juice)
Some Recipes Also Add a Little Sugar or Angostura Bitters
Pineapple Slice (For Garnish)
Maraschino Cherry (For Garnish)

Combine all ingredients except garnish in a blender and blend. Pour into those cute tall stem glasses. Garnish with the pineapple slice and maraschino cherry. Serve immediately.

S'More Pizza

This pizza should be cooked on a little hotter stone than most to cook the dough before the marshmallows burn.

1 Dessert Pizza Dough
3 Tablespoons Caramel Sauce (warm to at least room temperature so it drizzles easily)
1 1/4 Cup Miniature Marshmallows
3/4 Cup Chocolate Chips
1/2 Cup Graham Cracker Crumbs

Preheat pizza stone to 450 degrees. Roll out the dough on floured board. Sprinkle cornmeal on peel. Gently shake extra flour off dough and put on peel.

Drizzle caramel sauce evenly over dough. (Do not spread, it will just pull the dough out of shape.) Arrange chocolate chips and marshmallows on dough. Make sure marshmallows are not too close to the edge. Sprinkle cracker crumbs over the top.

Cook on 450 degree pizza stone until dough is done, about 4 minutes.

Pair with Tobin James' Liquid Love, a late harvest Zinfandel which goes wonderfully with chocolate. (Or is it the chocolate that goes wonderfully with the wine? I'll need to try them again to decide...) Tobin James Cellars is about as far east on Highway 46 as you can go and still be in Paso Robles. They have a fun old west theme in their tasting room. Their website is www.tobinjames.com.

Upside Down Cheesecake Pizza

Messy to eat, but delicious! Don't be surprised if people need silverware to eat this one.

1 White Pizza Dough
1 Tablespoon Cornmeal
8 Ounce Package of Cream Cheese (or Mascarpone)
1/2 Cup Fruit Compote (Recipe in Sauce Section) or Preserves
1/2 Cup Graham Cracker Crumbs

Preheat pizza stone at 450 degrees. Roll out the dough on floured board. Sprinkle cornmeal on peel. Gently shake extra flour off dough and put on peel.

Spread fruit compote on dough. Soften cream cheese by whipping or microwaving for 20 or 30 seconds. Spoon over compote and spread evenly. Sprinkle graham crumbs over the pizza.

Cook on 450 degree pizza stone until dough is done, about 6 minutes.

Pair with Adelaida Cellars Ice Wine, a sweet wine with flavors of fruit and honey. Traditional ice wines are made from grapes that have frozen on the vine, which doesn't happen in California. Adelaida freezes the pressed juice and separates out the water to get the right sugar levels. Adelaida Cellars is another family owned vineyard in the mountains of west Paso Robles. Adelaida's website is www.adelaida.com.

Too Many Cooks

Our block can put together a group ready for just about any kind of fun on very short notice, which is very handy for food experimentation. If we need opinions on a new pizza topping combination we can have half a dozen testers over in 5 minutes. Low on inspiration? Call John and Grace and they will happily sprinkle arugula, almonds, and feta onto a pizza to try. Mike and Maria will suggest an enchilada pizza.

Somewhere along the way we developed a following. If we mention that we will be barbecuing pizzas, word spreads and we end up with an enormous crowd. It has become our favorite type of party. Everyone has so much fun! For us a small party is a dozen people and a typical pizza party is two dozen or so.

The largest number of pizza cooks we have had is somewhere around seventy-five. Even I will admit that this is a bit excessive. If you only make dough at the ratio of one pizza to two guests, you will be kneading until the cows come home the day before. And guests tend to be unhappy with that ratio, everyone wants to make one of their own. The pushing and shoving at the topping table quickly gets out of hand. Then the pizzas stack up waiting to be cooked on the barbeque, because we can only cook two at a time.

When preparing for this huge (seventy-five plus people) pizza party I did not have enough large bowls to make the dough for the forty pizzas I estimated we would need. So I let the first batch rise for only about two hours and then put the dough into plastic bags for the next day, storing them on baking sheets in the oven which was off.

I thought it would not rise much more and could finish rising in the bags, there was half again as much room for the dough. This was NOT a good idea. Pizza dough is not to be trusted. The dough more than doubled in size and began trying to get free, like the Blob in a bad sci-fi movie.

Some of the bags unzipped and let the dough creep out over the edge of the baking sheet and drip down through the oven rack to the bottom of the oven. What alerted me to the problem was a bag that did not quietly unzip, but instead burst with a loud pop.

Mathematically, with two pizzas cooking at a time and five minutes or so per pizza, we could supposedly cook two dozen pizzas per hour. Which should be fast enough. However math fails us, because that level of efficiency is not compatible with the alcohol consumption of a macho cook.

Four pizzas will be ready to cook at one moment, and then there will be no pizzas ready at another. Some pizzas will cook slowly, either because they are thick-crusted and loaded with toppings, or because the stone has cooled from opening the barbeque frequently.

In any case, a reasonably sober cook can only produce about fifteen pizzas an hour on a two pizza stone. Once the cook is drunk, which doesn't take long, since barbequing is hot, thirsty work, the pizza production drops precipitously. Substitute cooks can be used, however their alcohol consumption probably began at the same time as the original cook's, and will increase drastically once they are standing over a hot barbeque.

Party Tips

The wonderful thing about barbeque pizzas is that they are great as a party activity. Everyone can assemble one that is just what they want. Although remind them to stay close when it is cooking. Pizzas tend to disappear as soon as they are cut.

It does take a little while for people to learn how to put the pizzas together and become comfortable experimenting. Show a person or two and ask them to please help show others. It is a great way to get everyone talking. Our friends are forever trying to outdo each other with the most unusual creations.

You will need a large area for assembling pizzas. I like to use three tables: one with a board to roll out dough. The second with sauces and cheeses. And the third with toppings grouped by type; meats in one area, seafood in another, veggies, and so on.

The topping table should have a small cutting board for those who want to chop toppings into smaller pieces. Remember that each table will need clear areas to set peels down on. I prefer to put these tables out on the patio. Pizza making is an extremely messy activity.

Near the cooking area, but far enough that the cook can breathe, should be the serving area with a large cutting board for pizzas, and perhaps a second table for side dishes. Cut pizzas into lots of small pieces – everyone wants to try everything. Warn guests to pay attention when their pizza comes off the barbecue – many times the person who made the pizza doesn't get a taste.

At this point, you are probably out of tables. But you need a few more so people have somewhere to sit and eat. Just place them out, away from all the other tables. You don't want a pizza dropped on someone. (Although people do look awfully funny covered in pizza toppings.) Our granddaughters knocked an uncooked pizza into someone's lap. Yes, it landed topping side down. They always do.

A few people to help run the party will make things go much smoother. It takes some coaching to get first timers started, but once they get the hang of things the assembly area can get crowded. You will want one person in charge of the assembly area at all times; helping to show people what to do and finding more spoons, flour, etcetera as needed. The barbeque needs constant watching and someone needs to be in charge there too. We rope in the guests as much as possible.

Make sure you have lots of peels for pizza assembly. The one time we tried to make do with three peels (one for the barbeque and two for assembling) we had guests at each other's throats. Can you imagine the food fight that could develop? Marinara sauce, olives, smoked salmon... Yuck!

When someone asks what they can do, tell them. Send them in search of more spoons. Ask them to chop onions. Have them put more wine in the cook's glass. Ask them to take over for the drunk cook. I enjoy a party more when I feel like I helped make it a success and most of our friends say the same. We also know our neighbors well. Mike starts doing dishes when he is drunk, so we make sure he gets lots of wine at every party. We lose an occasional wine glass, but it is well worth having so much of the cleanup done.

There is a long list of suggested ingredients to have on hand for a pizza party in the checklist. This list contains everything needed to make all the recipes in this book, which would be practically impossible in any one party. Use the list to make sure you have a couple of things from each category. We always ask everyone to bring one or two of their favorite toppings. That way we concentrate on dough, the main cheeses, sauces and a few basic toppings.

Clean Up

When the party is winding down try and remind everyone to take home what they brought. I have found that with my friends there is more food in my house after a party then there was before the party. Trying to fit it all in the fridge is a challenge.

Use Ziploc bags and freeze as many leftovers as you can for the next time you make pizza. Each pizza size dough ball can be refrigerated or frozen in plastic bags. They are never as good as fresh dough, but work pretty well once they return to room temperature.

Sauces can also be frozen in small plastic containers. Remember to label everything, once frozen it is hard to tell the difference between marinara and enchilada sauce. Wheat dough and dessert dough look fairly similar too. I write on the bags with marker.

Warning: the marker comes off on surfaces while defrosting so put paper towels under bags when you take them out of the freezer. My pink countertop has a lavender "Wheat" upside-down and backwards that I hide under the tea kettle.

There will be a lot of peels and cutting boards covered in flour, corn meal and pizza crumbs. Do NOT rinse flour and corn meal down your sink. Scrape as much as you can into the trash. Plumbers are not cheap any day and they charge extra on weekends. Wash the peels and cutting boards with warm soapy water and rinse well. Do not let the wood sit in water for any length of time and make sure they have plenty of air circulation to dry quickly after washing. If the wood stays wet it may warp or crack.

Let any food stuck to the pizza stone cook to ashes and then turn the barbeque off. Brush the ashes off the stone and leave the stone to cool – probably overnight. Stones can take many hours to cool. You can remove the stone from the barbeque the next morning and wipe it with a damp cloth to remove any leftover ashes.

Pizza Party Checklist

If you have asked guests to bring their favorite toppings to your party then you should focus on having enough dough, sauces and cheeses for the number of expected guests. For all the other toppings you can supply the amount needed for a small group. With what the guests bring this should be plenty of food. First time pizza party attendees usually bring traditional toppings like pepperoni, so if your group is mostly new to pizza experimenting you should concentrate on the exotic ingredients.

Dough

If you are serving other foods with pizzas (salads, appetizers etc.) then a third to half a pizza per person should be more than enough. If pizza is the only food (and with salad, main dish and dessert pizzas this is a good option), then plan about one pizza per person. When making dough, one cup of flour will make one pizza.

All Purpose Flour
Almond Meal
Basil
Cinnamon
Cooking Spray
Corn Meal
Garlic
Italian Seasoning
Olive Oil
Oregano
Salt
Sugar
Thyme
Vanilla
Whole Wheat Flour
Yeast

Sauces and Spices

For a small group of ten to twelve people, two or three sauces should suffice. Each pizza only uses a few tablespoons of sauce. Add another sauce for every 10 people or so.

Alfredo Sauce
Balsamic Vinegar (or Peach Balsamic Vinegar)
Barbecue Sauce
Biryani Paste
Blue Cheese Dressing
Buffalo Wing Sauce
Cajun Spice Blend
Caramel Sauce
Chili Powder
Chimichurri Sauce
Enchilada Sauce
Honey
Hot Sauce
Marinara Sauce
Mustard
Olive Oil
Orange Infused Olive Oil
Pesto Sauce
Ranch Dressing
Salsa
Sriracha Sauce
Steak Sauce
Thai Sweet Chili Sauce
Tomatillo Sauce
Tomato Sauce
Wine Reduction Sauce
Sauce Ingredients:
Balsamic Vinegar
Basil
Berries
Butter
Fresh Basil Leaves
Fresh Rosemary
Garlic

Heavy Cream
Honey
Italian Parsley
Lemon Juice
Olive Oil
Oregano
Parmesan
Pepper
Pine Nuts or Walnuts
Red Wine
Romano Cheese
Shallots
Sugar
Thyme
Worcestershire

Cheeses

Shredded Mozzarella is a must for a pizza party. You will average about a cup per pizza and there are four cups in a pound. So a five pound bag can make up to twenty pizzas.

Blue Cheese
Buffalo Mozzarella
Cheddar or White Cheddar Cheese
Cream Cheese
Feta Cheese
Four Cheese Blend
Goat Cheese
Mascarpone
Shredded Mozzarella Cheese
Parmesan Cheese

Pepper Jack Cheese
Provolone Cheese
Romano Cheese

Meats and Proteins

For most meats you'll use about a quarter of a pound per pizza. So for a small group of ten people, start with a pound each of two or three different meats. Add another two pounds of meat for every ten people invited.

Bacon
Carne Asada
Chicken
Corned Beef
Eggs
Ham or Canadian Bacon
Hamburger
Italian Sausage
Louisiana Sausage
Meat Balls
Pastrami
Pepperoni
Pulled Pork
Refried Beans
Roast Beef
Salami
Shrimp
Smoked Salmon
Steak
Tri Tip

Vegetables

Onions and bell peppers are a must. If you have time to chop the vegetables before the party then pizza assembly will go faster. But people are also fine with chopping as they assemble so don't stress if you run short on time.

Arugula Lettuce
Avocado
Bell or Mini Peppers
Capers
Chipotle Peppers
Dill Pickles
French Fried Onions
Fresh Basil
Fresh Cilantro
Fresh Dill
Fresh Garlic
Green Onion
Jalapeno Peppers
Lettuce
Marinated Artichoke Hearts
Mushrooms
Olives
Pasilla Chilies
Red Chili Peppers
Red Onion
Sun-Dried Tomatoes
Tomatoes, fresh or canned diced

Sweet Stuff

The bare minimum is one fruit and some chocolate. Most people will be full by the time that you start making dessert pizzas so you'll only need to make a few. But once they have tried dessert pizza expect them to save room at future parties. Fresh fruit is best, canned can be used if it is well drained.

Bananas
Brownie Mix
Brown Sugar
Canned Peaches
Chocolate Chips
Chopped Macadamia Nuts
Cinnamon
Dried Cherries
Dried Cranberries
Dried Figs
Fruit Preserves or Compote
Graham Crackers
Mandarin Oranges
Maraschino Cherries
Mini Marshmallows
Nutmeg
Pears
Pineapple
Port Wine
Powdered Sugar
Raspberries
Rum
Shredded Coconut
Sliced Almonds
Sugar
Whipped Cream

About the Author

I was supposed to spend my life lounging on the French Riviera with a fancy cocktail in my hand, but somehow I got turned around and ended up in California with a glass of wine instead. Which is pretty darn close, except for that pesky working thing.

I'm past that wonderful, awful stage of raising kids. My husband of 30 years, Greg, and I are now into that really fun spoiling grandkids part of life. (Fill them full of sugar, tire them out and spoil them rotten. When they become totally impossible, hand them back.) We also have an assortment of rescued pets and a small vineyard in the backyard.

As a member of the California Writers Club, I'm enjoying writing and sharing my jokes and stories with others. I'm hoping one day writing will replace the blasted job.

Some of you have read this hoping to understand the workings of this author's mind. Let me clarify for you: This author is a few sandwiches short of a picnic. Why do you think I had to make all those pizzas? There just weren't enough sandwiches to go around. Not to mention a banana split sandwich just doesn't sound appetizing.

Happy Grilling!

About the Cartoonist

Jack Russo grew up in the San Fernando Valley in the 1960's with a steady diet of Mad Magazine and the works of R. Crumb. His irreverent humor displays a total disregard for the opinion of the reader, and no topic is off limits. He is pretty much a whack job with a pen, and can turn a blank piece of paper into a potential lawsuit in just a few minutes. How did he become this way? We think that either he was dropped on his head when he was a baby or there was too much mercury in his fillings. He has worked for a utility company since 1983 and more of his cartoons can be seen at http://gascartoons.com.

Recipe Index